SELECTED
Writings
VOLUME 1 ♦ 1974-1999

SELECTED Writings

VOLUME ONE

1974 – 1999

Shaw Clifton

Salvation Books
The Salvation Army International Headquarters
London, United Kingdom

ISBN 978-0-85412-831-0

Cover design by Berni Georges

Published by Salvation Books
The Salvation Army International Headquarters
101 Queen Victoria Street, London EC4V 4EH, United Kingdom

Printed by UK Territory Print and Design Unit

Also by Shaw Clifton:

What Does the Salvationist Say?
(London, UK, The Salvation Army, 1977)

Growing Together
(London, UK, The Salvation Army, 1984), with Helen Clifton

Strong Doctrine, Strong Mercy
(London, UK, The Salvation Army, 1985)

Never The Same Again
(Alexandria, USA, Crest Books, 1997)

Who Are These Salvationists?
(Alexandria, USA, Crest Books, 1999)

New Love – Thinking Aloud About Practical Holiness
(Wellington, New Zealand, Flag Publications, 2004)

Contents

Author's Introduction

These two volumes of writings from 1974 - 2010 are offered as a means of placing before a wider readership various articles and papers which hitherto have mostly been confined either to the pages of *The Officer* magazine, which has an officially restricted circulation, or to those in senior leadership in The Salvation Army.

Volume 1 consists entirely of some my early articles in The *Officer*. Volume 2 ranges more widely and comes right up to date, often dealing with key matters of international Army policy.

I record warm thanks to Lieut-Colonel Laurie Robertson, Literary Secretary at International Headquarters, for his helpfulness in getting these volumes into print, and also to Major Leanne Ruthven who helped to dig out the earlier materials from *The Officer* magazine.

My wife, Helen, and my three children – Matt, Jen and John – have been consistent sources of loving encourgement, as have my children-in-law, Marcus and Lynne, by their prayers. My Private Secretary, Major Richard Gaudion, has given splendid help with characteristic cheerfulness.

I dedicate these pages to my Saviour, Jesus Christ, and to his people known as Salvationists.

Shaw Clifton Ph.D
General

London, October 2010

CHAPTER 1

Martin Luther and the Priesthood of all Believers

[Recent years have seen an increase among us in the use of the expression 'the priesthood of all believers'. It is a beautiful concept. The great Martin Luther coined it in the 16th century to express the deep – and in his day radical – truth that none of us needs an intermediary to approach God. Each believer is his or her own priest. Despite this clear and simple meaning, some have come to misuse the phrase, making it a slogan for diminishing the role of a separate order of clergy or of officers, thinking mistakenly that the phrase is a battle cry which means: 'Anyone can do anything within the church!' Luther would have been puzzled by this distortion of his concept. In 1974, as a new Lieutenant, I felt honoured when the editor of The Officer *magazine, the then Major (later Colonel) Will Clark, graciously accepted an article from me for publication. It was about Luther's famous concept. This was my first ever article to appear in* The Officer. *Because of the misconceptions – see above – being aired in some Army circles about Luther's concept, I had this article republished in* The Officer *magazine late in 2010.]*

The idea of the priesthood of all believers is central to the Protestant-Attestant tradition in which we stand, and it should be useful to examine some of its implications. So together let us look back to 1520 and to the earlier stages of the European continental Protestant Reformation to encounter briefly the remarkable mind of Martin

1

Luther. Radical and revolutionary in his theological outlook, he is adjudged by history to have been a thinker of genius.

Luther published three famous treatises in 1520, each of which contributed in a major way to the Reformation. It is in *The Freedom of a Christian Man* that we find a succinct statement of the doctrine of justification by faith alone, the touchstone of the Reformation, gleaned by Luther from Paul's epistles as expounded by Augustine. The companion doctrine, that of the priesthood of all believers, is to be found in *An Address to the German Nobility*. This therefore is where we must focus our present attention. Luther developed the doctrine under the pressure of controversy, feeling compelled to assert it although he was himself an ordained priest. The intention of the *Address* was to urge Emperor Charles V and the ruling classes in Germany to initiate moves which would lead to the reform of the Roman church. However, says Luther, Rome had entrenched herself behind three high 'walls' which were keeping long overdue reforms at bay. The first part of the *Address* is therefore an attack by Luther upon these three 'walls', three specific claims to privilege made by Rome.

Among Salvationists today these issues are no longer a matter for debate. If we think about them at all we take for granted the non-Catholic view. Yet we are free to do this only because of Luther's stand and the subsequent work of consolidation by the other sixteenth-century reformers like Huldrych Zwingli and John Calvin.

Luther's chief weapon of attack against the claims to privilege made by Rome was the doctrine of the priesthood of all believers. Firstly, he challenged Rome's claim that the secular authorities had no jurisdiction over her and, having made clear his doctrinal position with regard to the relationship of clergy and laity, he urged the secular powers of his day to act without fear toward the ecclesiastical personages of Rome. The political issue here is not our immediate concern. What is instructive for us is the argument Luther uses; this argument hinges on the priesthood of all believers.

He says that it is specious to attempt, as the Romanists did, to classify Christians on the one hand into a religious category consisting of ordained persons and on the other hand a secular category made up of the laity: 'For all Christians whatsoever really and truly belong to the religious class and there is no difference among them except in so far as they do different work ... that is St Paul's meaning in 1 Corinthians 12:12.' Luther goes on to say that clergy and laity alike are all equally Christians since they have one Lord, one gospel, one faith. He writes, 'The fact is that our initiation into Christ consecrates us all without exception, and makes us all priests.' This is an explicit statement of the priesthood of all believers.

However, it is vital to undetstand that Luther is not advocating the abolition of a separate clergy. He is asserting simply the availability of the same divine grace for all believers, whether the believer is a member of the clergy or not.

So within the Christian community Luther rejects the division into a superior clergy and an inferior laity. He asserts that when a bishop ordains a man (or woman) he simply acts on behalf of the entire congregation, 'all of whom have the same spiritual authority'. Every Christian is regarded as being as much a priest as a man (or woman) who has been ordained by all the bishops and popes in Christendom! This does not mean that within the Christian community different functions overlap. It means that any distinction between clergy and laity is not derived from special grace available to one and not the other, nor from the different qualifications of each, but from the different tasks and roles laid upon them. Neither clergy nor laity enjoys special grace- privileges one over against the other; instead each is bound to the other by a tie of mutual service.

Suppose, says Luther by way of illustration, that a group of Christian laypersons were to find themselves in the middle of the desert without an episcopally ordained priest among them. If they agreed that one of their number should fulfil the office of preaching, teaching, etc., that person would truly be a priest in the fullest sense but, because of the need for orderliness in the church, they would not all undertake such tasks.

3

Luther then turns to the Roman doctrine that ordination as a priest bestows upon a man certain 'indelible characteristics' so that if he is later unfrocked and deposed he is nevertheless still different from a mere layperson.

Luther denies the truth of this and dismisses it as a mere human invention and regulation. He urges that the status of a priest among Christians is that of an officebearer; while he (Luther assumed priests would be male and hence the male pronoun here) holds the office he exercises it; if he is deposed he retains none of the status relating to the office. 'Hence we deduce that there is, at bottom, really no other difference between laymen, priests, bishops, or in Roman terminology, between religious and secular, than that of office or occupation and not that of Christian status.' A little further on we read, 'Those called priests, bishops and popes, possess no further or greater spiritual dignity than other Christians.'

Having demolished the first 'wall' behind which he accuses Rome of hiding, Luther takes less time to deal with the other two. The second 'wall' is Rome's claim that only the Pope is competent to expound and interpret Scripture. Again he turns upon this claim the doctrine of the priesthood of all believers. 'Each and all of us are priests because we have the one faith, the one gospel..., why then should we not be entitled to taste or test and to judge what is right or wrong in the faith?' He then cites Paul in 1 Corinthians 2:15: 'The spiritual man makes judgements about all things, but he himself is not subject to any man's judgement.'

He deals in similar fashion with the third 'wall' of Rome, the claim that the Pope alone has authority to summon a council of the whole Church to effect reforms. Luther argues that the secular authorities also have such a right, 'especially since they are also fellow Christians, fellow priests, similarly religious, and of similar authority in all respects.' We must understand this in the context of Luther's belief that all secular authority is divinely instituted by God, but here again he takes the priesthood of all believers and allows it to go to its logical conclusion.

The implications of the priesthood of all believers for Salvation Army officership are clear. Crucial to the tradition in which we stand, the doctrine is incompatible with any idea of there being a difference in kind, or in spiritual standing before God, between officers and others. Our relationship to Luther is one of lineal descent. Had he somehow been asked to pronounce upon a theology of officership he would not have been able to reply in terms of 'privileged apostolic succession' or 'special calling'. Perhaps he would have challenged the premise behind the very phrase, 'theology of officership', and would have denied that the distinctiveness of officership is to be found in theology at all.

Rather it is found in the unique covenant into which a person enters if he or she wishes to become an officer. Only those about to be commissioned as officers make this covenant, often in addition to other covenants made earlier (soldiership, marriage, etc.). Also, the distinctiveness has to do with special function within the Body of Christ. Luther argued passionately in favour of a separate (not theologically superior) clergy, for the sake of good order. He never imagined a church in which non-ordained (non-commissioned) persons would exercise functions or roles reserved to clergy.

The content of his *Address* of 1520 makes it certain that Luther, to whom we owe so much, could never have used theology to point up any basic or grace-related distinction between clergy and laity. Any difference was one of function. In fact he saw it as the role of theology to demonstrate precisely the absence of any distinction of spiritual status between clergy and laity. The only distinction Luther recognised was confined to the classification of roles, not any distinction of divinely bestowed grace.

CHAPTER 2

Aspects of Christian Ethics

Major Will Clark, Editor of The Officer, *graciously accepted from me six articles about ethical issues and published them in the March - August issues of 1975. This was my first full series to be used in The Officer. At the time Helen and I – with our first child, Matthew, aged two – were Lieutenants and stationed in Rhodesia at the Army's Mazowe Secondary School. In writing these straightforward articles it was my hope that they might prove a stimulus to others to think, speak and write on social ethics, an area of concern crying out for a Salvationist voice. At about this time the Army was beginning to produce various positional statements on such matters but this work was in its infancy. Soon after the series appeared I received word from Major Clark that International Headquarters intended to use the articles for a short book. This appeared shortly thereafter, entitled* What Does The Salvationist Say? *A few months later General Clarence Wiseman visited the Rhodesia Territory and came to Mazowe. The General spoke to me in most gracious terms about the little book and expressed the Army's thanks for it. I was moved by this. An expanded version of it appeared later in 1985 entitled 'Strong Doctrine, Strong Mercy'. It would have been possible to update the articles for this present publication, but I have resisted that thought and now offer them here as a snapshot in time, with introductory comments to place them in context. The main principles enunciated remain, I believe, as applicable as ever.*

What Makes Christian Ethics Christian?

The danger of accepting uncritically some of the traditional Christian attitudes to the moral and ethical issues of our time is an obvious one. The danger lies not in the acceptance as such but rather in the blind and unquestioning manner of it. To fail to question is to fail to analyse, which in turn means a failure to understand fully the grounds upon which our moral stands are taken.

When such stands meet opposition, the unquestioning mind has to resort to brave but bold dogmatism. In contrast, the questioning mind, having searched (often painfully) for truth before accepting it, can meet opposition with informed and reasoned argument. The uninformed sloganiser is asking for opposition; the searcher for truth can disarm the opposition.

Let us be specific. As Christians we take a stand against indiscriminate abortion, euthanasia, racialism, the devaluing of marriage and other moral evils. But do we stop to ask ourselves why we hold such views? We must be able to defend them intelligently. In an age of controversy we must be armed with reasoned arguments if the debate with secular man is to be joined. In these matters, he will not be swayed by slogans. Accordingly, subsequent articles in this series will attempt to analyse and assess the rational bases for the Christian stance on some leading moral issues of the day. The aim is to reach a deeper understanding of Christian ethical attitudes. Whilst our destination is orthodox, the route may hold surprises!

To study ethics is to study standards of behaviour. To study Christian ethics is to study Christian standards of behaviour as influenced and conditioned by Christian theology. Defending successfully any Christian ethical point of view involves being aware of what it is that gives Christian ethics its distinctively Christian character. Let us try to tease out this specifically Christian factor.

First, we have to make a broad distinction between, on the one hand, an autonomous system of ethics and, on the other, a non-autonomous ethical system. The former is said to be autonomous in that it does not rely on any extraneous authority for the moral standard set up. No attempt is made to justify a given moral standard in terms of, for instance, what conscience, God or an innate and universal moral law might dictate. Instead, it is claimed that an action is morally right because it will increase the sum of happiness in the world (a 'utilitarian' ethic), or because it will, by man's unaided efforts, bring nearer the ideal human society (a 'humanist' ethic).

We may note, therefore, two things about an autonomous ethic: (a) it seeks to justify conduct only in terms of its consequences; (b) it does not depend on adherence to any religious beliefs.

It follows that the Christian ethic is a non-autonomous ethic. It differs from an autonomous (and usually atheistic) ethic in that, whilst it gives full consideration to the consequences of all action, it does not seek to justify that action solely in terms of its consequences. Rather, the act, or the morality of it, will be justified in religious terms. Another way of putting this is to say that Christian ethics appeals for its validity to an authority beyond the action itself.

It is in determining the identity of that authority that we begin to see clearly what makes Christian ethics Christian. We have reached the heart of the matter. The question we must answer is: 'Who or what constitutes the authority upon which Christian ethics is based?'

However, before offering an answer to this, we have to pause to deal with a logically prior question, namely, 'In the area of morals, is it rational to allow any place at all for the concept of an "authority"?' This question is usually put by those who argue that to yield one's actions to some authority extraneous to oneself is to abandon responsibility for those actions. It is claimed to be an attempt to pass the buck which, in the sphere of moral responsibility, is thought impossible since morality is so personal and subjective.

If this argument is valid, we have to re-examine the primary assumptions of Christian ethics. However, the following observations may be made. Since ethics is to do with decisions on how to act, and since only persons make decisions, it follows that, if there is to be an authority of some sort in Christian ethics, it will be a person and not an office or institution.

A person becomes an authority in a particular field (a) if he has more practice in it than others, and (b) if he has available to him more of the relevant data than others. In other words, it is having more experience or more knowledge that constitutes a person an authority. In the field of ethics or morality the data consists of 'moral facts'. These show whether an act is right or wrong (and ought not to be confused with 'ordinary facts' which serve merely to show whether a statement is true or false). If it is possible for one person to have more knowledge than another of the relevant moral facts then the notion of a person who is an authority in morality is not irrational. To claim it is irrational is to claim that we act contrary to reason whenever we seek advice from another on any ethical matter. Clearly, such a claim is absurd.

So much for the preliminary question. Let us return to the heart of the matter, namely, to seek the identity of the authority on which Christian ethics is based. It cannot be the Church, since that is not a person but an institution. Neither may we say, without further explanation, that the authority in question is the Bible, for that is not a person but a book (albeit the Book).

Rather, the basis of Christian ethics and the authority for any act rightly called Christian is the person and teaching of Jesus Christ. Being divine, he is author of the moral standard; as sinless man, he is also our perfect Example. He and he alone stands before us as our exemplary ideal. This in turn means an authoritative role for Scripture since our primary knowledge of Jesus is found there and without it we should soon lose our way. But in God's self-revelation to man it is necessary to see the role of Scripture as instrumental. The substance of the revelation is Jesus Christ. Christ is the content, whilst Scripture is the means.

This is why we must identify Christ, and only Christ, as the authority for Christian ethics. No other has discerned truly and responded perfectly to the divine, moral demand. Only he can claim to have offered the Father total obedience (John 17:4). Only he knows all there is in human nature (John 2:25).

We may therefore say that what makes Christian ethics Christian is its Christ-centredness. It is a Christocentric ethic, summed up in phrases like 'following Christ' or 'the imitation of Christ'.

It is precisely at this point that Christian and secular ethics part company. As Christians, we may admit the feasibility of a secular ethic but never its superiority. On the contrary, we hold that not only is it possible to have an essentially religious idea of the moral life, but that such an idea is preferable to the secular alternative in that it does justice to the spirituality of humans and meets their total needs.

Keith Ward (in *Ethics and Christianity*) makes a similar point but rightly goes on to enter a caution: 'It does not follow that Christians will be morally better than non-Christians; for religious morality, like any other, can become an oppressive and relentless taskmaster. I would agree with the opponents of Christianity in thinking that there can be few things more abhorrent than a fanatical and intolerant pursuit of religious dogma; but no systems of morality are immune from the perversity of their adherents. The Christian conception in itself seems to me both more adequate to the moral situation of men and also more morally desirable.'

Let it be stressed that what Ward calls 'a fanatical and intolerant pursuit of religious dogma' is worlds away from the true Christian ethic. Yet none can deny that in both past and present the ethic of 'the imitation of Christ' has occasionally degenerated into a rigid and legalistic adherence to obscure biblical injunctions, often taken out of context and interpreted literally. To treat the words of the New Testament, and in particular the words of Jesus, as a set of rules is to treat them with a legalistic superficiality. It is to mistake words of life for words of law. This was the mistake of the Pharisees (John 5:39,40).

It was T.W. Manson who, in explaining 'the imitation of Christ', developed the analogy of the trainee musician who listens to and watches the expert instructor. In the earliest stages of his training he copies closely the teacher's technique. But, given time and practise, he gradually develops his own style and flair so that the day comes when he can perform creatively whilst nevertheless remaining within the principles and influence of his training. So it is with the follower of Jesus. As he grows in Christian grace and wisdom he finds himself acting creatively in his moral life yet always remaining true to the example and teaching of his Master.

The need for creative moral reasoning, in harmony with the life and teaching of Christ as recorded in the Gospels, will become apparent when, in future articles, we discuss some of the pressing moral issues of our times. On some of these Scripture has no specific 'command of the Lord' and hence the need for creative reasoning in keeping with Christ's spirit. The problem is not new; Paul faced it when offering ethical advice to the Corinthian Christians (see I Corinthians 7:25).

Nevertheless, Scripture presents to us the cornerstone of the Christian ethic, Christ himself, who is lacking in nothing since all that is the Father's is his (John 16: 5). His words and teaching bring life and creativity (John 1:3,4; 5:24, 25; 6:68). Moreover, he has promised us the Comforter who will teach us all things (John 14: 26) and who will guide us into all truth (John 16:13).

In view of this, dare we be less than adventurous and creative in our thinking? God calls us to be his fellow-workers and the work God does is never less than creative.

A Christian Approach to Divorce

[From The Officer, *April 1975. This was written at a time when the laws of divorce all over the world were undergoing radical change, not least in those countries whose legal systems had been strongly influenced by English Common Law, for example, the United States of America, Canada, Australia, New Zealand. A global trend emerged which saw the old fault-based laws on divorce give way to simpler no-fault laws based on the concept of 'the breakdown of the marriage', regardless of the conduct of the spouses toward one other. These legal transitions were eventually to produce highly significant changes in the Army's regulations governing marriage and divorce. With the courts no longer willing to pronounce upon the relative 'guilt' or 'innocence' of the divorcing parties, Army leaders responsible for handling marital breakdown among officers and others were left with little to guide them as to the moral culpability, if any, that should rightly be apportioned between the spouses. Balanced regulations were introduced which took these changes into account and which also emphasised strongly the pastoral dimensions.]*

In many countries we are constantly confronted with rising divorce statistics and so it will do no harm at all to remind ourselves at once that happy and successful marriages outnumber those that eventually break down. But the sad truth is that for as long as there have been marriages there have been failed marriages.

This article will trace the recent development of English divorce law (which should be of interest to officers both here and overseas) and examine two of the relevant New Testament passages.

To understand divorce it is important to appreciate marriage as a legal concept. The classic definition of marriage in English law was laid down in 1866: 'Marriage, as understood in Christendom, may ... be defined as the voluntary union for life of one man and one woman to the exclusion of all others.' Every word in this definition is crucial. The parties to the marriage are said to have entered into a contract to marry, that contract being satisfied by the solemnisation of the

13

marriage. There is thus created in law a specific relation between the parties. Mutual rights and duties arise and the parties have conferred upon them a new legal status, that of being 'a married person'.

If this then is marriage, the parties are said to be divorced upon the dissolution of the marriage bond and are deprived of 'married' status. The last decade or so has seen rapid change in the divorce laws of England. The Matrimonial Causes Acts 1950-1965 were based on the idea of the 'matrimonial offence' and the giving of a remedy to an 'innocent' spouse against a 'guilty' spouse. P.M. Bromley (*Family Law*) expressed the view of many when he said, 'To insist that divorce should be available only if a matrimonial offence has been committed lays stress upon the symptoms of breakdown rather than on the breakdown itself.'

So 1966 saw two major statements on divorce law reform. The first was *Putting Asunder*, a report by a group set up by the Archbishop of Canterbury. This concluded that the 'matrimonial offence' concept should be replaced by the 'breakdown of the marriage' as the sole ground for divorce. It advocated (as a safeguard) a judicial inquest in each case. The second statement was *Reform of the Ground of Divorce: the Field of Choice*, issued by the Law Commission of England and Wales. This analysis saw as impracticable some of the suggestions of *Putting Asunder* but went on to say that the aim of a good divorce law should be 'to buttress, rather than undermine, the stability of marriage, and when, regrettably, a marriage has irretrievably broken down, to enable the empty legal shell to be destroyed with the maximum fairness and the minimum bitterness, distress and humiliation.'

This resulted in the passing of the Divorce Reform Act 1969 which took effect on January 1, 1971 and enacted that the sole ground for divorce would be 'that the marriage has irretrievably broken down'. This Act is now re-enacted in the Matrimonial Causes Act 1973 which forms the basis of English divorce legislation as it stands today. One vital provision of the 1973 Act is that attempts must be made at every stage in the proceedings to effect reconciliation between the parties. The solicitor (attorney) is duty bound to give his client details of where to obtain professional marriage guidance and the divorce proceedings can be adjourned at any stage if reconciliation seems likely. Strict provisions are laid down which safeguard as far as possible the interests of any children affected by the divorce.

Christians, of course, will want to seek guidance on moral issues less from the law than from the pages of Scripture and so any Christian view of divorce must give an adequate account of the New Testament statements on the subject. However, here we meet a major problem. Both Mark and Matthew report the same basic saying of Jesus on divorce but with sufficient variations one from the other to suggest that the writers of these Gospels were to some degree confused as to what exactly Jesus had said. Let us look first at Mark 10:2-12.

Mark makes the conversation between Jesus and the Pharisees stem from the question: 'Is it lawful for a man to divorce his wife?' In view of Deuteronomy 24:1-4, which recognises plainly the legality of a bill of divorce, it seems that the Marcan form of the question is unlikely in an historical sense. The parallel question in Matthew 19:3 is given in a form historically more probable: 'Is it lawful to divorce one's wife for any cause?' Matthew therefore makes the topic of conversation the scope of a bill of divorce whereas Mark makes it the initial validity of any bill of divorce.

In Mark the Pharisees then go on to summarise the position under Mosaic law, namely that Moses allowed bills of divorce. The point of Jesus' reply is that Moses was making a concession to human weakness. Jesus says that their 'hardness of heart' (or refusal to obey God's will) had resulted in a frustration of the divine purpose summed up in Genesis 2:24: 'Therefore a man leaves his father and his mother and cleaves to his wife, and they become one flesh.' In other words, Genesis 1:27, which distinguishes male from female, has to be qualified by Genesis 2:24 which envisages the creation by marriage of a bond which is as indissoluble in God's eyes as the blood tie between a man and his parents.

Mark 10:10-12 has Jesus pronouncing that divorce is wrong whatever the reason. The underlying assumption seems to be that all divorce is a sin against God (in view of Genesis 2:24) and moreover that a subsequent remarriage would constitute adultery, thereby adding a second sin to the first.

We have already noted that the question put to Jesus in Matthew 19:3-9 differs from the one he answered in Mark. A second difference between the two accounts is that Matthew stresses the contrast between the word 'command' as used by the Pharisees in verse 7 and the word 'allowed' as used by Jesus in verse 8. That is, Jesus emphasises that Moses intended not a normative command but a permission or concession where God's ideal will had been frustrated by human weakness. Perhaps the most striking (and most baffling) difference between the two Gospel accounts occurs in verse 9. Mark 10:10-12 records a total prohibition by Jesus upon divorce but here in Matthew we are told that Jesus allowed an exception in the case of 'unchastity' (Greek: *porneia*). The scope of the exception is far from clear since *porneia* could mean either pre-marital fornication or post-marital adultery. Most commentators prefer the second meaning.

One thing at least is clear. The irreconcilable statements at Mark 10:10-12 and Matthew 19:9 make it impossible to 'read off' a divorce ethic from the Synoptic Gospels. If the Early Church found it difficult to discover the mind of Christ on the issue of divorce, then how much more of a problem it is for us!

Nevertheless, the two passages discussed so far are not altogether empty of guidance. We can extract from them in general terms some idea of what Jesus thought. It would appear that he distinguished between two different orders (ethical frameworks) in the world of human affairs. The first order is that indicated by the words 'from the beginning' (Mark 10:6 and Matthew 19:8). This is the order of God's eternal purpose for man in which the rule is: 'no divorce'. Even Moses cannot alter this. The second order is that signified by the phrase 'for your hardness of heart' (Mark 10: 5 and Matthew 19: 8).

This is the order of things as they now stand in an imperfect world and for which the rule is: 'divorce within limits'. This second order is less than ideal and has to be seen as a concession to realism. It falls to the Church to work out for itself, just as Moses had to work them out in his day, what the proper limits must be when God's original 'Creation-intention' (that all marriages would be healthy and lifelong) is perceived to have been frustrated by human frailty. Despite such frustration, despite human failure, the Church is called to continue to witness to the eternal validity of the first order rule by retaining the 'for life' vows in the marriage ceremony.

Some Christian bodies, e.g. the Church of England, have interpreted the Gospel statements on divorce in a way that prohibits the remarriage in church of any divorced person. On the other hand the Free Churches and The Salvation Army are prepared – in certain closely examined circumstances – to officiate in the marriage of a divorced person. Each case is considered on its merits. No automatic bar to remarriage is felt to exist merely because of there having been a divorce. No doubt these divergent attitudes both spring from a desire to safeguard the institution of marriage. However, the signs are that the rigid approach of the Anglicans is changing to something more flexible. Even as this article is being written, it is reported in London's *The Times* that the Church of England is to open up discussion once again on this very issue.

The Christian Church is commissioned to bring to wrecked and wounded lives the healing power of the Gospel. Sometimes a divorce wrecks and wounds as nothing else can. When this happens the Church must be on hand to bring healing and renewal. In certain cases these may come about only in a second marriage.

Some Christians have felt genuine concern at the recent trends in the reform of the divorce laws of England, but the question which arises is whether Christians can reasonably expect the civil law to be a model of Christian ethics when Christians are now in a minority in society and in any case cannot agree amongst themselves what the law ought to be. We have to ask ourselves, as C.S. Lewis puts it in

Christian Behaviour, 'how far Christians, if they are voters or Members of Parliament, ought to try to force their views of marriage on the rest of the community'. Is it a Christian's duty to try to make divorce difficult for everyone? Is marriage best safeguarded by forcing couples to live together in an empty relationship from which love has long since vanished?

Perhaps we should begin our thinking on these questions by admitting frankly that most people today are not Christians and therefore cannot be expected to live Christian lives.

C.S. Lewis advocates the establishing of two distinct kinds of marriage. One would be for all citizens and organised by the State. The other would be for Christians only and supervised by the Church. 'At least this would allow us to recognise', says Lewis, 'which couples are married in a Christian sense and which are not'. It is an idea worth exploring.

Meanwhile, Christian men and women must witness to the sacramental nature of marriage, marriage as a means of grace and healing:

'Let us go deeper
you and I
for we belong together
and love's image dwells within
God's you and I
we must explore
in prayer
and find the real each other
awareness growing all the time
for each is for the other
in the likeness of Christ's mind.'

(*Exploration into Love*, Malling Abbey, 1970.)

Abortion

[From The Officer, *May 1975. Few subjects arouse emotions like that of abortion. The strongest feelings can be found on both sides of the abortion debate. I will never forget arriving as the new Divisional Commander in Boston, USA in mid-1995 in the immediate aftermath of shootings at an abortion clinic in that famous city. The religious life of Boston was dominated by Roman Catholicism – half of all church-going Bostonians were Catholics) – and by Bernard Cardinal Law, later to suffer disgrace (and the sale of his impressive residence to meet legal costs) over his handling of the child abuse scandal in his diocese. He had at first urged Catholics to demonstrate in public against the abortion clinics. After the shooting he rapidly reversed his stance and urged restraint. It was too late. I recall vividly my first meeting with him and other Christian leaders in the city to discuss the shooting. The Cardinal seemed surprised, but quietly impressed, that the Army had anything to say on the matter. The fact is that abortion has never been merely an academic or theoretical one for the Army because we have hospitals and other medical services and therefore must constantly determine policy on medical matters. The same applies in relation to our counseling services across the world where clients may seek abortion advice. Also many Salvation Army corps officers encounter those with pressing, abortion-related pastoral needs. It is worth remembering also that sometimes different parts of the Army world see key ethical issues differently. Abortion is one such example. Salvationists in the USA, for example, would be inclined to espouse a more conservative view than many in Europe or in Australasia. We can live with these differing emphases. They do not go to the heart of the matter which is the stance one takes on the status and value of the human fetus, something on which the global Army remains united. Readers can access Army ethical-positional statements on abortion and other topics on various Army international and territorial websites.]*

Thirty-seven thousand abortions were performed in Great Britain under the terms of the Abortion Act 1967 in the first year of its operation. The figure is now in excess of 150,000 such abortions annually. It was against this background of an ever increasing number of abortions, many apparently for no more than social reasons, that in January, 1973 *The Officer* magazine published a 'Statement on Abortion', approved by the General as the official view of The Salvation Army.

This statement rightly urged 'that a Royal Commission or similar body be set up to study fully the social and ethical aspects of abortion, with a view to a basic revision of the 1967 Act'. It was also stated that 'the unborn child is a potential person from the moment of conception, and a potential member of a family and of society. . . .' This view is the corner-stone of the Army's stand against abortion on demand and therefore provides the best starting point for any discussion of the ethics of abortion.

The Army's view that the fetus must be regarded as a potential person from the moment of conception can be traced back at least as far as Tertullian, a brilliant North African theologian who lived from about AD 160 to about AD 220. He rejected the idea that the fetus should be seen merely as a growth on the mother's body and therefore removable at will. He said that the moments of quickening and birth played no role in the fetus becoming a person for all the essential conditions of personhood were present as soon as conception took place.

Today the view of Tertullian on the status of the unborn child is the one we adopt, for the life of the newly-born baby differs not in kind, but only in environment, from the baby's life in the womb. Furthermore, it is the view presupposed by the Common Law of England which, when capital punishment was practised, forbade the hanging of a pregnant woman on the grounds that to hang her would be an assault upon the innocent life of her unborn child. Recent Common Law decisions have been welcomed which recognise the legal right of a child to sue for compensation for injuries received prior to birth. Tertullian's view (and the Army's) is also the one which gives us the broadest possible definition of human life. It must be in the interests of all of us to seek a wider, not a narrower, definition of life.

It is worth mentioning at this point a special issue in 1973 of the Roman Catholic journal, *Month*. The entire issue was devoted to the problem of abortion with contributions from experts in medicine, psychiatry, sociology, law and ecology. The opening article stated bluntly that Christians can best protect unborn children by broadening the grounds on which they argue against abortion. The writer went on to accuse many of his fellow Catholics of 'rhetorical overkill', by which he meant that they had waxed eloquent in presenting religious arguments against abortion when addressing largely non-theists, i.e. persons with whom an argument based on a belief in God would cut no ice at all. The article saw the status of the fetus as the central issue in the abortion debate and reiterated the view that the unborn child should be seen as alive, as an individual, and as a person in its own right. All of this lends strong and welcome support to the Army's view.

If the status of the fetus is that of a person in its own right, what may rightly be said to be the value of the fetus? Should we place on it an absolute value, that is, should we preserve it at all costs? It would seem not, for we do not place such a value on human life in general. We admit that there are exceptions to the rule that human life is sacred, as in the case of self-defence. Nevertheless, we have to give the fetus an extremely high value, as high as that given to human life in general, so that the burden of proving the morality of ending the life of a fetus in any given case falls squarely on the one claiming the exception to the general rule of the sanctity of life.

This brings us to the question of individual cases. In what sort of circumstances should an abortion be seen as morally permissible? The Army's view is that 'abortion should continue to be legalised on adequate medical grounds, both physical and psychological, but not for social reasons'. So a pregnancy may reasonably be terminated when the physical or mental health of the mother is seriously threatened. The United Kingdom Abortion Act 1967 provides for this but goes much further, further than Salvationists would wish. It permits an abortion if the pregnancy involves risk to the health of other children of the mother whether or not her own health is threatened. It is not easy to envisage occasions when an abortion would be justified on this ground.

The Act also allows a termination when there is a substantial risk that if the child were born it would suffer from such physical or mental abnormalities as to be seriously handicapped. The wise person would be very slow to pronounce upon the morality of aborting in a case of such abnormality, but it could be said that this provision in the Act ignores the sophistication of a modern community which should be equipped to care adequately for handicapped persons. It leaves out of account also the love and devotion which such persons may both give and inspire. Today medical science can, by means of a fetoscopy or amniocentesis, diagnose defects in the fetus well in advance of the birth. To assume automatically that abortion is always morally justified where a defect is found is to overlook that the quality of human life is much more than physical perfection.

Many would argue in favour of abortion in cases where the child is conceived in unethical circumstances such as rape or incest or even where the mother is below the age of consent. Dogmatism on these suggestions is out of place. Perhaps the best approach here is 'every case on its facts', always remembering that society's interests are best served if we restrict abortion to narrower rather than broader limits.

Widespread abortion must eventually have a dehumanising effect on any society that encourages it. Non-Christians with permissive views on abortion have sometimes claimed that the desire to restrict the practice goes hand in hand with 'Christian narrow-mindedness' on sexual matters in general. There is evidence, however, that it is natural to the human species as such to restrict abortion fairly narrowly and that aversion to the artificial termination of pregnancies is not limited to Christian countries. Deep concern about the morality of some abortions cannot be dismissed as the result of 2,000 years of Christian obscurantism since such concern is found even among the non-Christian Japanese. A survey carried out in 1972 shows that 59 per cent of Japanese non-Christian women thought abortion 'very wrong' whereas only 8 per cent found 'nothing wrong' with it. Of women who had aborted (over one million a year) 82 per cent said that they experienced feelings of guilt afterwards.

Research has also been conducted into the relation between abortion and subsequent psychological disorder in the women concerned. In a society which pretends that abortion is a trivial matter or merely a minor operation to be undergone as a means of easing the social inconvenience of a pregnancy, the women are being asked to live out a contradiction. On the one hand they are expected to assert life (by sometimes bearing children), but on the other they are expected to suppress life (by sometimes aborting). Living a contradiction results in conflict and psychological disorder. In London in February, 1973 *The Sunday Times* reported a Californian study which found that in the short term the effect of an abortion was simply relief that the problem of the pregnancy had apparently been solved. But in the longer term the story changed dramatically, for within a few months over half the women in the survey were in need of psychiatric help. The pattern was one of 'acute depression, an inability to work, clinging and immature dependence on parents, and in some cases promiscuity where before there had been steadiness'.

Other independent surveys confirm this frightening picture. As time passes, the need in Britain for a Royal Commission grows ever more urgent, but also called for is a mammoth programme of social education. This would seek to combat the habit of mind which, in some circles, leads from the recognition of an unwanted pregnancy straight to a shrill demand for an abortion.

Race Relations

[From The Officer, *June 1975. Modern readers may find the title of this article – not the topic – a little dated. Nowadays we might speak of inter-ethnic or inter-cultural relations. The Army has, since the 1970s, developed highly effective multi-cultural ministries departments in some places, not least in the USA. Readers will also note my 1970s' use of the English term 'racialism', rather than the American 'racism' which has now become the universal word, with 'racist' overtaking 'racialist'. I was taught early in my life that English speaking Salvationists never use the word 'foreigner' when referring to fellow Salvationists from other lands and cultures. 'Foreigner' carries overtones of separateness, of someone alien, even occasionally a hint of intimidation arising out of otherness. An extension of this is found in the Army's banning of the word 'enemy' from all its literature in time of war. So in the Army we prize our God-given internationalism and will refer to 'a comrade from overseas' or will use other language which, while respecting healthy cultural differences, does not connote alienation. Readers will know that in the 1970s the attention of the whole world was drawn to the struggle against the apartheid system prevailing in South Africa. It was against that background that this short article was put together. In the month of its publication we were living and serving in Rhodesia and experiencing for ourselves what it felt like to be seen first as 'white' or 'black' or 'coloured' and only thereafter as human.]*

As an Army of the 'God of every nation', we have always taken pride in our internationalism. Bramwell Booth's declaration in 1912 is still true: 'The Salvation Army belongs to the whole world. It knows no nationality as such.' We can boast that the word 'foreigner' is not in our vocabulary and this in an age beset by problems of race relations.

The World Council of Churches defines racialism as 'ethnocentric pride in one's own racial group and a preference for the characteristics of that group, believing these characteristics to be biological and hence transmitted to succeeding generations'. An alternative definition might be: 'The theory that some race or races are inherently superior to others and the organising of a society or a political economy on that basis.' This second definition is more realistic in that it indicates the effect racialism has on the allocation of votes ('political'), jobs ('economy'), on intermarriage and population distribution ('society').

It is not new to say that the Christian aim is to build a society which accepts and glorifies the differences between the races without making a barrier of them. In international terms, the aim is harmonious co-existence. Where different races are found within one national boundary, the aim is integration, not assimilation. Integration permits an immigrant group to play a full and responsible role in society without loss of cultural or national identity. Assimilation, on the other hand, is the process whereby such a group becomes submerged or absorbed into society so that their cultural heritage is totally destroyed.

Most people seem ready to agree that racialism is immoral, but rarely do they say why it is so. Perhaps race relations could be helped if what seems to be a vague, inarticulate aversion to racial discrimination became instead a worked-out, explicitly grounded belief. Our hand will be strengthened if we establish clearly the principles from which we work.

On what grounds then does the Christian take a stand against racialism? In the opening article of this series reference was made to the imitative nature of Christian ethics: 'What makes Christian ethics Christian is its Christ-centredness . . . summed up in phrases like "following Christ" or "the imitation of Christ".' So our attitude to the issue of race relations will seek to imitate that of Christ.

Jesus was a Jew but as a member of that intensely nationalistic race, he rose above its narrowness and exclusivism, thereby incurring the anger and enmity of his fellow-countrymen. His sermon at Nazareth stressed that God's grace reaches further than the Jews liked to think: 'But in truth, I tell you, there were many widows in Israel . . . and Elijah was sent to none of them but only to . . . the land of Sidon' (Luke 4:25,26, RSV).

It is 'the world' to which Jesus came to bring light (John 8:12) and the same is true for his disciples (Matthew 5:14). Also, in the parable of the weeds among the wheat, the field is said to be the world' (Matthew 13:38).

Even the focal point of Jewish worship, the Temple itself, is to be 'for all the nations' (Mark 11:17). Similarly, the command was given to 'make disciples of all nations' (Matthew 28:19). In these words there is no hint that any one race is either superior or inferior to another. Indeed, the reverse is true. All nations are to receive the gospel, a gospel sounding its keynote of reconciliation.

Whilst imitative in character, Christian ethics is essentially theological. Christian behaviour is conditioned by Christian beliefs, or ought to be. Allowing doctrine to determine (albeit indirectly) our actions is sometimes called 'having the courage of our convictions'! So which Christian doctrines affect our thinking about race relations?

We need not look far. 'In the beginning' God created the heavens and the earth and said, 'Let us make man in our image, after our likeness' (Genesis 1:1,26). Here 'man' means 'mankind', the entire human species without exception. Of all the creatures, only humans are made in God's image. All humans are equal in their freedom to disobey the divine will and equal in their responsibility before God. Every human, whatever his or her race, bears the divine image. In the New Testament Paul calls human beings 'the image and glory of God' (1 Corinthians 11:7) and in passages like Matthew 25:40, 45 we meet the concept of the Christ in every man. Inasmuch as the racialist unjustly discriminates against a member of another race, he discriminates against Christ.

Closely linked with the Christian doctrine of creation is the Christian doctrine of the human race which teaches that all persons are equal in intrinsic worth. There are differences of course, but these are God-given and therefore good. 'God saw everything that he had made, and behold, it was very good' (Genesis 1:31). In the dispensation of Christ, potential barriers between people are reduced to trivialities for 'there is neither Jew nor Greek, there is neither slave nor free, there is neither male nor female' (Galatians 3:28). Above all, each and every member of the human race stands in need of grace. There is none free from sin and without a need to be forgiven. Grace deprives all of us of any claim to status.

This brings us to the doctrine of the atonement. Sin requires forgiveness which results in reconciliation. The reconciliation of man with God must lead to the reconciliation of man with man. Segregation on racial grounds denies a gospel of reconciliation. Is there a person for whom Christ did not die? Does Christ love some more than others? Questions like these need acted, not spoken, answers. Let the loving and accepting relationships of Salvationists around the world be a living testimony to the victory of Christ, the universal Reconciler.

Clearly, racialism is contrary to God's will for man whether the racialist has black skin or white. F.B. Welbourn, writing in *The Expository Times*, sums it up this way: 'To say, "I am black", "I am white" – to say even, "I am a Christian", if that is to be a member of a narrow and exclusive group – is false because it is less than the truth and dangerously hides the truth that, in Christ, we are simply human beings.'

As if to exemplify the internationalism of the Army, as these words are being written, the office of the Territorial Commander in Kinshasa, Zaïre, is occupied by joint Territorial Commanders, one black man and one white man. In Christ there is neither black nor white.

'Join hands then, brothers of the faith,
Whate'er your race may be;
Who serves my father as a son
Is surely kin to me.'

(John Oxenham)

Voluntary Euthanasia

[From The Officer, *July 1975. Recent years have seen this topic become more and more prominent in terms of media attention and public debate. Ever-advancing medical techniques provide opportunities for a person to be kept alive far longer than in the 1970s. The pro-euthanasia advocates have grown in number and in their ability to influence public opinion and legislation. 'Suicide clinics' are reported in Switzerland and, in other countries such as the Netherlands, we learn of family doctors regularly taking positive measures to end a patient's life prematurely, actions to which the law turns a blind eye. The human factors involved are deep and complex. Helen and I know from personal experience what it means to be called upon to consider the switching-off of a life-support machine for an elderly father or to approve the administration of analgesic drugs to an aged mother which will ease her pain but suppress her lung capacity and hasten indirectly her death.]*

It has been said many times that death as a topic of conversation is taboo nowadays. There is, however, a healthy and vigorous debate going on about euthanasia. The word euthanasia (the Greek prefix *eu-* means 'well' or 'beautiful' and the Greek *thanatos* means 'death') means literally 'a good death' or 'gentle easy death', but at the present time it has come to mean the deliberate killing of someone who is suffering from a distressing and irremediable disease.

That is the sense in which the term will be used in this article, which confines itself to a consideration of voluntary euthanasia. Euthanasia is said to be voluntary when the patient consents to being killed in order to escape the suffering an incurable disease may bring. It is the deliberate, requested extinction of a human life. Voluntary euthanasia stands over against the compulsory sort, when death is deliberately accelerated regardless of the wishes of the patient.

In most countries of the world the legal position with regard to euthanasia is plain. Whether voluntary or otherwise, it means killing. A doctor is no different from an ordinary subject of the realm regarding a right to kill a dying patient. Professor Glanville Williams, an expert on English criminal law, writes: 'Under the present law, voluntary euthanasia would, except in certain narrow circumstances, be regarded as suicide in the patient who consents, and murder in the doctor who administers; even on a lenient view, most lawyers would say it could not be less than manslaughter in the doctor, the punishment for which, according to the jurisdiction and the degree of manslaughter, can be anything up to imprisonment for life' (*Sanctity of Life*). If a doctor gives, for example, a fatal injection, he or she is almost certainly guilty of murder and it would be no defence that the victim consented, or was suffering severe pain, or would soon have died in any case.

In January 1971 the British Medical Association (BMA) published a report entitled *The Problem of Euthanasia*. This comes out strongly against euthanasia of any description. It tries to put the matter into a proper perspective by stressing at the outset that 'some of the emotion behind the demand for euthanasia lies in the belief that death will be peaceful and dignified only after a lethal injection'. The report, which represents the official view of the British medical profession, emphasises that the vast majority of deaths are peaceful, whatever the preceding illness, and that, contrary to popularly held opinion, even the majority of patients suffering from cancer die peacefully.

What kind of case is usually put forward for legalising voluntary euthanasia? The literature of the Voluntary Euthanasia Society in Britain offers two main arguments. Firstly, it is urged that incurable patients are occupying scarce hospital resources which should be used for patients who have a chance of recovery. This is true, but why is the killing of incurable patients seen as the answer? In the circumstances, our moral duty is to increase the facilities available. Euthanasia is the easy answer. Like most easy answers it is the wrong one.

Secondly, it is argued that to kill a suffering and incurable patient who requests it is the compassionate and merciful thing to do. Many are swayed by this argument. The use of words like compassion and mercy make it superficially attractive. However, a moment's thought will show where this kind of reasoning leads. If it is compassionate to kill a patient who is capable of consenting to euthanasia, it is logical to suppose that it is even more compassionate to kill one who by reason of an extreme condition is unable to consent. So we end up practising, not voluntary, but compulsory euthanasia. We thus find ourselves on a slippery slope to all kinds of horrors. Once we convince ourselves that it can sometimes be morally right to kill a person (in peacetime) against their wishes, we have begun to reverse the process of moral enlightenment which the centuries have unfolded. Moreover, such a view is incompatible with what the Gospels teach about the value and sanctity of each individual human life.

Let us look now at the positive case against euthanasia. Some of the arguments against it are religious (theistic) in nature and therefore appeal only to those with a belief in God. We shall outline first the non-theistic arguments, those which do not depend for their validity on any religious belief.

Firstly, there is the familiar 'wedge' argument. This has been touched upon already in discussing the logical implications of the pro-euthanasia case. There is considerable force in saying that voluntary euthanasia, once legalised, would be the thin end of the wedge which could open the door for even more questionable practices. We live in an age when long-standing moral standards are gradually being eroded. If the law gives its blessing to voluntary euthanasia it would simply hasten that process of erosion. Moreover, Christians recognise that man is sinful by nature and any weakening of respect for human life will eventually be exploited and abused.

A second argument highlights the risk of diagnostic or prognostic error on the part of the doctors. The medical profession is respected for its high standards of skill but there is still a real possibility of a wrong diagnosis or simply some confusion in the patients' records. Mistakes here, as with capital punishment, cannot be put right. Let the BMA report speak for itself: 'Medical diagnosis, even though carefully made and supported by many tests, will always contain an element of fallibility. A recommendation for euthanasia would have to be based upon a diagnosis of irreversible physical or mental illness. Mistakes would inevitably be made.'

Thirdly, the whole concept of voluntary euthanasia is beset with difficulties relating to the nature of the consent given by the patient. This consent must be voluntary. To be valid it must be made by a person of sound mind. Yet an expressed desire for death may be a sign of a mental illness, in which case the request for euthanasia would be rendered invalid. If consent is given prior to the onset of the fatal disease, it has to be consent in view of some imagined future distress. This raises the question of whether a person can ever truly consent to being killed on the basis of what he or she may or may not be able to tolerate at some future date. If, on the other hand, consent is given at the time the disease is actually being endured, there are still problems.

In March 1969 an ultimately unsuccessful Voluntary Euthanasia Bill was introduced into the British Parliament's House of Lords. The Bill stated that the patient must be of a 'responsible' mind at the moment of consent. Yet it also required the patient to be suffering from some fatal disease expected to cause severe distress or render incapable of rational existence. Can consent be real in such circumstances? It is hard to envisage how a responsible state of mind and intolerable suffering can coexist. If they cannot coexist, voluntary euthanasia is a nonsense, a contradiction in terms.

A fourth point in the case against euthanasia is that there is a sound and proven alternative to the killing of dying patients, namely, good pre-terminal care and the skilled use of analgesic drugs. Writing in London's *The Times* (November 1974) about euthanasia, Professor Symington, Director of the Institute of Cancer Research, states: 'Much can be done to relieve the physical, emotional and social distress that is encountered. Contrary to popular belief, the severe pain that all too often dominates extensive malignant disease can be alleviated, frequently abolished . . . the advocacy of euthanasia in such circumstances is increasingly irrelevant.'

In the same copy of *The Times* Dr R.G. Twycross, Research Fellow at St Christopher's Hospice, London, writes: 'It is important to appreciate that it is theoretically possible to relieve the pain in every case.... The all too often account of a person dying in agony after weeks or months of unrelieved pain should increasingly become a thing of the past.' Even Lord Raglan, the promoter of the 1969 Voluntary Euthanasia Bill, has admitted that the skilled and careful use of analgesic drugs in the care of the dying is a compelling argument against euthanasia. Agreeing with this view, the BMA has pointed out the need for more instruction in such matters to be given to doctors during their medical training. The need is for a change of emphasis and in attitudes rather than a change in the law.

Finally, but briefly, there is the whole question of the effect legalised euthanasia might have on doctor-patient relationships. Each consultation might arouse mistrust in the patient's mind. As Dr Duncan Vere says: 'The role of healer would be clouded by the role of death-bringer' (*Voluntary Euthanasia*).

We turn now to some theistic (grounded in a belief in God) considerations which might weigh heavily with Christians. If God is the source of human life, the reasons for ending it must be more compelling than human consent or convenience. If seen as suicide, voluntary euthanasia might be rebellion against God and a denial of his providence. It presupposes that there is such a thing as a totally useless state of human life. It is born of hopelessness and despair, both of which are contrary to the spirit of the gospel. Any sentient state can still bear hope. The Christian sees the weakening of this physical life as a step toward a new life with God. Except in cases of accidental or sudden death, we think of the experience of contemplating the approach of death as a desirable, even necessary preparation for the life that is to come.

For the Christian, death points to our utter helplessness before God and our ultimate dependence upon him. Faith requires us to wait upon God in patience. A request for euthanasia is no less than a refusal to trust a loving God. P.R. Baelz has called it 'an embracing of death for its own sake, a form of self-justification, a desertion to the enemy'. It is to abandon a waiting in hope in favour of a final act of despair.

The Just War

[From The Officer, *August 1975. When this article was put together, I had little idea that in later years my interest in the ethics of warfare would develop so strongly. This culminated in a decision taken at about the time of my 40th birthday to embark upon a close analysis of The Salvation Army's global actions and policies in time of war. The research was rewarded with a Doctor of Philosophy degree by the University of London, King's College. I am still indebted to my leaders in the Army who encouraged me to do this work and who ensured the costs were met. It seems as though wars and rumours of wars ever increase. Insurgency warfare is now commonplace. The tactics of terrorists have grown more and more sophisticated, including the hijacking of aeroplanes and the deployment of suicide bombers. The little article below, compiled when I was about 29 years old, seems as relevant today as it was when written. The issues remain as intractable.]*

This article touches on issues so large that it must be mainly descriptive rather than evaluative. It will attempt to outline the idea of the just war as it has arisen in the history of Christian thinking. Probably the two most noteworthy names in this field are Thomas Aquinas and Hugo Grotius.

A clear distinction must be made between the idea of a just war and that of a so-called 'holy' war. The latter plays no part in traditional Christian teaching which has always seen war as essentially unholy. It is crucial to grasp that the 'just war' doctrine attempts to show those circumstances in which the evil of war might be endured in preference to some even greater evil of injustice or oppression.

Before outlining the doctrine, something must be said about the way the New Testament is often used when Christians debate the ethics of war. Non-pacifists and pacifists alike (there are Salvationists in both categories) claim to find support in Scripture for their particular view. Matthew 5:38-48 is often seen as binding Christians to an absolute policy of non-violence, whatever the circumstances. At the turn of the century Robert E. Speer commented on this view as follows: 'Jesus does enjoin brotherly love and long-suffering, but he does not thereby mean to secure to injustice a perfectly free field when it has power to work its will. The position of some opponents of war reduces itself to this – that bad men may resist bad men, but good men may not. Jesus did not teach this view' (*The Principles of Jesus*).

It seems plain that Christians are called to resist evil. The issue arises over the means to be adopted. So the following is the relevant question: 'Is war ever a legitimate means by which Christians may resist evil?' In Romans 13 the Apostle Paul clearly recognised that governments (as over against private citizens) have not only a right but a positive duty to resist evil by the sword. It is futile to argue that this applies only to non-Christian governments. To quote Speer once more: 'It is not possible that God should intend a heathen government to prevent evil, but a Christian government to permit it.'

When discussing the teaching of Jesus in relation to this, it is a mistake to inject into his words a legalism not intended when they were first spoken. He lays down principles, not rules. He advocated turning the other cheek (Matthew 5:39), but in John 18:22 there is no hint that he offered his other cheek when struck unjustly. Furthermore, the Gospels frequently tell us how he took active steps to avoid capture and death until the occasion was right for him to submit. The attitude of Jesus would seem therefore to be: 'Resist when it is right to resist, but submit when it is right to submit.'

This is certainly how the advocates of the just war doctrine have interpreted his teaching. They say that the Christian is committed to peace but he strives for other social goals as well. He seeks justice, security and freedom. If he gives peace an absolute priority whatever the circumstances, it will sometimes mean that exploitation and oppression go freely on their way.

Thomas Aquinas was a 13th century Italian monk whose influence upon theology and philosophy continues to the present day. He sets out his theory of the just war in his *Summa Theologica* relying heavily on the earlier views of Augustine. According to Aquinas, the foremost factor in a just war is that it must be initiated by proper authority of the sovereign. War is not for private citizens to wage. Secondly, there must be sufficient cause for the war. That is, an enemy may be attacked if he deserves it. Aquinas adopts Augustine's definition of a 'just cause': 'One that avenges wrongs, when a nation or state has to be punished for refusing to make amends for wrongs inflicted by its subjects, or to restore what it has seized unjustly.' Thirdly, a just war is one waged with a 'good intention'. The intention must be to secure the common good and ultimately to bring about peace. Aquinas says that even if a war is waged by the right authority and for a just cause, it will be unjust if the intention behind it is wicked.

The aim of this theory is to place limitations upon the waging of war. Aquinas stresses that there is something essentially unchristian in shedding blood, even in a just war. But he accepts the necessity of sometimes having to resist a greater evil by means of the lesser evil of fighting a just war.

After Aquinas there was little development in the just war doctrine until the 16th century and the rise of the great nation-states. The work of Francisco de Vitoria (1480 to 1546) and Francisco Suarez (1548 to 1617) paved the way for that of Hugo Grotius, a Dutch jurist born in 1583 and sometimes hailed as 'the father of international law'.

In his treatise, *On the law of War and Peace*, he starts by assuming that a thing is lawful for a Christian if it is not unjust. He says that he finds no clear teaching in the Gospels about war and so he argues from general principles: 'The courage which defends our country from barbarians abroad, or the helpless from harm at home, or society from robbers, is complete justice.' He agrees with Aquinas that war is essentially inhuman and that only the 'highest necessity' or the 'deepest charity' could justify it.

Discussing pacifism, he says that each person has an absolute right of conscientious objection so that, even in a just war, any

Christian unwilling to fight should be excused. Grotius saw it as particularly holy to abstain from lawful military service. He argued that it is more pious (in the best sense of the word) to give up our rights even if we would be justified in going to war. He adds, however, that this does not mean that it would be blameworthy to assert our rights and enter upon a just war in the same circumstances.

His treatise dealt not only with the question of when it is right for a Christian to go to war but also with that of how a just war ought to be conducted. Two main principles emerge, the principles of discrimination and proportion. The former seeks to protect non-combatants from direct attack, It maintains that military action should, in its primary thrust as well as in its subjective purpose, discriminate between directly attacking combatants and non-combatants. This is not the same, however, as saying that civilians should never knowingly be killed. It is a question of one's primary target.

The principle of proportion requires that only those means should be used which are a necessary precondition of achieving the end in view. If an enemy can be stopped by some means short of killing, then that means is the one to adopt because it involves the lesser evil. The end justifies the means (since nothing else can!) – but not any means.

These principles of discrimination and proportion are still regarded today as fundamental to the moral conduct of a war. Yet it is increasingly difficult to see how they can always be applied to modern conditions of warfare. The line between combatants and non-combatants has been blurred so that not only is the man in uniform regarded as a legitimate target but so too is the civilian worker who manufactures the soldier's weapon. This happened in the Second World War, a war in which the two basic principles outlined above were virtually abandoned. The obliteration bombing of Dresden on the one hand and London or Coventry on the other bears witness to this fact.

This trend is strengthened by the advent of atomic and nuclear devices which have to be used without the ability to select pinpoint targets. They are 'all or nothing' weapons. Henry Nelson Wieman was right to say that the first atomic explosion 'cut history in two like a knife'. Similarly, we have to agree with the assessment of John Macquarrie that 'modern warfare has taken on characteristics which make it demoniacally dangerous'.

However, there is a matter of more immediate urgency. The main problem today facing not only Christian moralists but moralists in general is to work out an ethic for counter-insurgency warfare. What has the Christian to say about the morality of the means employed in fighting terrorists in, for instance, Vietnam or Northern Ireland? The terrorist fights from behind or amongst the civilian population. His is a subversive war. He hits and runs. He thinks it is better to strike and run away and live to fight another day. So far his tactics have succeeded. At the time of writing, the United Kingdom has been stunned by the callous bombing of innocent citizens by terrorists in Birmingham. Three bombs, 20 dead, 200 injured. How then is it possible to mount a morally acceptable counter-terrorist operation when often the enemy is a child with a bomb or a housewife with a shot-gun?

We have space here only to ask the question and thereby highlight the issue. It is an issue of vital importance for our time. The just war doctrine and its precepts seem of little practical help in combating terrorism. Must we then sink to the tactics of the terrorist and reply in kind? Answers are urgently needed and Christians are as obliged as anyone else to provide them. The Church is all too often accused of failing to give a clear moral lead, but modern insurgency warfare is one area in which we could so easily fail.

What at least is clear is that Christians must seek and support the peaceful settlement of disputes whenever it is possible. We must oppose those who reject the relevance of spiritual factors when it comes to policy-making. Equally, we must oppose those who are unrealistic enough to ignore completely the material considerations.

And we must never forget to uphold against all other claims the vocation of those who are known as pacifists and who renounce violence even in the highest cause. Such souls may not constitute the loaf, but we should fear the day when they are no longer allowed to be the leaven.

CHAPTER 3

John Calvin and Self-Denial

[From The Officer, *January 1976. Events in Europe in the 16th century leading to religious and civil upheaval and known as the Reformation have long intrigued me. During theological studies at King's College, University of London as a cadet I was glad to soak myself in the literature and lives of the leading Reformers including John Calvin. In 1974 the University graciously awarded me the Relton Prize for biblical and historical theology. That could not have happened but for the largeness of mind shown toward me by Army leaders – including the then Lieut-Colonel Alistair Cairns and Major Lyndon Taylor – who allowed me to combine cadet studies with more demanding and formal theological studies beyond the training college campus at Denmark Hill, London. Having previously soaked myself in the study of the law, there was now opened up to me a whole new world of hitherto unmet concepts and academic personalities. I found it deeply enriching and, contrary to the expectations of some in the Army, profoundly affirming of my personal faith.]*

Absorbing the writings of the 16th century Reformers is a stimulating pastime. Some of John Calvin's ideas are hard for Salvationists to take, so it is pleasantly surprising and not a little encouraging to find in his *Institutes of the Christian Religion* (1559) considerable emphasis given to the concept of self-denial.

There can hardly be an officer who has preached at Self-Denial time without taking pains to impress upon the congregation the spiritual (as distinct from the pecuniary) aspects of Christian self-denial. Calvin's watchword, 'We are not our own', could be adopted by us all. In Book Three of the *Institutes* in the chapter headed, 'A Summary of the Christian Life: of Self-Denial', we find this: 'We are not our own; therefore, neither is our own reason or will to rule our acts and counsels. We are not our own; therefore, let us not make it our end to seek what may be agreeable to our carnal nature. We are not our own; therefore, as far as possible, let us forget ourselves and the things that are ours. On the other hand, we are God's; let us, therefore, live and die to him (Romans 14:8).'

Calvin sets up self-denial as 'the leading principle' of the Christian life. It is an 'accurate method' by which we can fulfill the law of our divine Master. Hence the cardinal exhortation in Romans 12:1 (NEB): 'Present your very selves to him: a living sacrifice. . . .' This, says Calvin, puts it beyond dispute that the true Christian is dedicated to God's glory, not his own. Scripture (Calvin's entire theology is built on what he calls 'the Scripture system') enjoins us to lay aside private regard for self. We should divest our minds of excessive longing for wealth, power, human favour and instead bring all things to the disposal of God. Calvin continues, 'That self-denial which Christ so strongly enforces on his disciples from the very outset (Matthew 16:24) as soon as it takes hold of the mind, leaves no place, first, for pride, show and ostentation; or, secondly, for avarice, lust, luxury, effeminacy, or other vices which are engendered by self-love.'

The reformer then states his firm opinion that where self-denial has failed to take hold there will be found either the worst vices or a mere appearance of virtue, vitiated by a depraved longing for applause. He flings out a challenge! 'Show me, if you can, an individual who, unless he has renounced himself in obedience to the Lord's command, is disposed to do good for its own sake!' Assuming the tone of the pulpit, he goes on, 'There is a world of iniquity treasured up in the human soul. Nor can you find any remedy for this than to deny yourself, renounce your own reason, and direct your whole mind to the pursuit of those things which the Lord requires of you and which you are to seek only because they are pleasing to him.'

Calvin's head is not in the clouds. He recognises two great obstacles which stand in the way of self-denial. The first is 'ungodliness', which he sees as meaning everything at variance with a true fear of God. The second is 'worldly desires', which include 'all the lusts of the flesh'. Expounding Titus 2:11-14 as a mini-sermon on Christian living, he argues that the New Testament reduces all our actions as Christians to three main branches – sobriety, righteousness and godliness. Sobriety denotes chastity, temperance, the pure and frugal use of worldly goods and the patient endurance of poverty. Righteousness comprehends all the duties of fair dealing and giving every man his due. Godliness separates us from the world's pollutions and draws us heavenward in true holiness of mind and heart.

From his own experience (which was riddled with disputes and confrontations with critics both Protestant and Roman Catholic) Calvin is able to say that it goes very much against the grain to prefer others before ourselves and even actively to seek their advantage before our own. In Romans 12:10 and Philippians 2:3 we have 'commands which our mind is utterly incapable of obeying until its natural feelings are suppressed'. Can it be that God really wants us to count others better than ourselves? All others? In all circumstances? That's right, says Calvin. It's an extreme remedy for an extreme dose of selfishness! 'For so blindly do we all rush in the direction of self-love that . . . the vices with which we abound we both carefully conceal from others, and flatteringly represent to ourselves as minute and trivial, nay, sometimes hug as virtues.' Later he points out how frequently we denigrate in others those same qualities which in ourselves we regard as virtues, all in some frenzied attempt to remain one up!

For all this there is no other remedy than to pluck up by the roots 'those most noxious pests', self-love and love of one-upmanship

(Calvin's phrase is 'love of victory'). Accordingly, the Scriptures teach us that the endowments God has given us are not our own (1 Corinthians 4:7). The only way is the way of self-renunciation and wholehearted devotion to others. It is the heart of Christian self-denial, says Calvin, 'spontaneously to yield our own right, and resign it to another'. This is the law of love. The only right way is that which is regulated by love. Nothing else will do. In all this Jesus is our perfect example.

In one of his most eloquent passages Calvin admits that we meet few who seem worthy of our love and esteem. 'But', he writes, 'Scripture tells us that we are not to look to what men in themselves deserve, but to attend to the image of God which exists in all and to which we owe all honour and love.' Even more does this apply to our fellow Christians because in them that image of God, marred and distorted by the Fall, has been renewed and restored by the Spirit of Christ. Seen in this spiritual light, there is none who is a stranger, there is none to whom we have no ties of duty, there is none who is lowly or unworthy, for the Lord has, as it were, substituted himself in their place. Only in this way can we attain to what is altogether against nature. The image of God in men draws us irresistibly by its beauty and dignity to love and embrace what would otherwise repel and revolt us.

Is it just a theory? Did Calvin practise what he preached? Following his death in May, 1564, one of his closest associates in Geneva, Theodore Beza, wrote: 'On that day, then, at the same time with the setting sun, this splendid luminary was withdrawn from us. His life was an example of the Christian character which it is as easy to slander as it is difficult to imitate.'

CHAPTER 4

We believe in God

[This was a Lenten sermon preached as a Lieutenant in Salisbury Cathedral, Rhodesia early in 1977 at the invitation of Colonel Richard Atwell, Territorial Commander. Today this Anglican church is known as Harare Cathedral, Zimbabwe and is sadly a focus of controversy and dispute. I was grateful to Colonel Atwell for trusting me to represent the Army and also to the territorial General Secretary of that day, Lieut-Colonel Ron Cox for similar affirmation. Under General Eva Burrows, Ron Cox became the Chief of the Staff in succession to Commissioner Caughey Gauntlett. It was an honour later to serve at International Headquarters in the 1980s and to be directly accountable to all of these distinguished leaders. In 2009 Helen and I made an official visit to the numerically huge Zimbabwe Territory in our capacities as the Army's world leaders. It was a visit full of memories and nostalgia, intensified by the political and economic difficulties through which Zimbabwe is still passing. It was wonderful to witness the fidelity of the Salvationists under the fine leadership of Commissioner Venice Chigariro and also to be accompanied and warmly supported during the visit by the Africa zonal leaders based at International Headquarters, Commissioners Amos and Rosemary Makina. During a short period of personal time on that occasion Helen and I walked through the streets of the city and came to the cathedral. Seeking admission we were denied entry on the pretext of 'security'. In fact the church was closed down due to factional disputes. The sermon was published in The Officer *in March 1977.]*

Others have spoken on 'God as Father' and on 'God as Creator'. I shall therefore concentrate my remarks upon the word 'believe'. I want to speak about belief or faith – the nature of faith.

First, two biblical passages. In Isaiah's call to faith in Isaiah 26:1-4 (AV) we are told, 'Thou dost keep him in perfect peace, whose mind is stayed on thee, because he trusts in thee.' Next, in Deuteronomy 28:64-66, we find a sharply contrasting picture of a faithless people who have 'no ease', 'no rest' and the 'trembling heart' typical of anyone who is without a stabilising faith in God.

Now I have deliberately placed these passages at the beginning of my remarks because I am convinced that what the Bible says about faith must be determinative for the Christian believer. Nevertheless, let us be realistic and admit at once that the biblical concept of faith cuts no ice at all with today's secular man man who allows his life to be governed solely by logic and reason.

'It's not logical to believe in God!' this man cries. He is never slow these days to challenge us and to demand proof that our belief is valid. I do not think for a moment that it is out of place for us, when met with such a challenge, to play the rationalist at his own game. Why should we not be every bit as analytical as he is?

Now the God in whom we believe is not bound or limited by human reason and so we must be slow to offer logical proofs of his existence. Perhaps there are no such proofs, but we Christians must never allow to go unanswered the allegation that our belief in God is unreasonable or not intellectually respectable. Let us not yield to the propaganda of the unbeliever! He would have us think that it is only the atheist or agnostic who is being intellectually rigorous. He would say that the person who believes in God is a creature of sentiment, someone who lives by feelings and turns a blind eye to what reason and logic dictate.

We will never accept this charge! Do not believe the propaganda of the rationalist. Have none of his belittling comments. The attitude of the atheist is no more reasonable and no less reasonable than that of the Christian. 'Faith' or 'non-faith', these things are not to be judged by the standards of logic at all. Belief is reasonable and so is unbelief. There is evidence enough to support either stance on purely logical grounds.

What we need to do is consistently remind ourselves that God does not ask us to be logical or reasonable at the expense of our spiritual faculties. Rather, he asks us to be trusting and faithful, full of faith.

He asks us to offer him not merely intellectual assent, but a trusting spirit. He asks us to depend upon him for our very lives! He demands that we should, quite literally, believe and live.

I have suggested that perhaps there are no logical proofs for the existence of God. Please allow me to retrace my steps a little and make reference to the famous ontological argument of Anselm, the 12th century Italian monk. If I were to speak plainly, I would confess my fascination with this argument and the fact that it convinces me totally. There are three stages to the argument:

(a) If God exists, he has to be defined as 'that than which nothing greater can be conceived'.

(b) It is greater to exist in actuality than to exist merely as the figment of someone's imagination.

(c) If God is the greatest thing that can be conceived, he must exist in the greatest possible way, that is, in actuality and not merely as a figment of the mind.

It is worth the effort of thinking this through at leisure. We have much to learn from Anselm's approach. First of all, he recognised in faith, that is, with his spiritual faculties, that God exists. Then, and only then, did he seek to establish the fact of God's existence by the power of reason. In other words, reason is to be subordinated to faith. Anselm's attitude was one of 'faith seeking understanding'. He asserted: '*Credo ut intelligam*' ('I believe in order to understand'). In Anselm we find typified the kind of faith that leads on to intellectual enlightenment.

Ultimately, however, our belief in God will rest not on proofs, however compelling they might be, but on knowledge. Just as it is possible to have personal knowledge of a friend or a spouse, so it is possible, given time and frequent contact, to have personal knowledge of God. This is the knowledge possessed by the biblical writers. With such knowledge they found logical proofs irrelevant or superfluous and so we find no attempt in the Bible to prove God's existence by logic.

It is knowledge such as this which is our true goal in life. It is such knowledge which brings the 'perfect peace' of which Isaiah speaks.

May I quote from an excellent little book written recently by Canon David Edwards and entitled *What Anglicans Believe*? There he offers this advice: 'Think about God much more than about yourself, want him more than you want anything for yourself, but try to make sure that there is love in your heart and peace in your mind, so that you are not distracted by any foolishness. Say to God: "If you are real, give me the eyes to glimpse your reality." Ask God to show himself to you as he really is, even if it means showing you that you will have to change your own ways of thinking and behaving.'

Finally then, let us reassert, as we approach Easter, that we dare to believe in God. Yes, we have the effrontery to believe in a self-sacrificing God, the God who gave us Jesus Christ, the God who gave himself for us that we might believe and live.

CHAPTER 5

The Claims of Jesus – The 'I Am' Sayings of John's Gospel

Through the years I have found myself more and more at home in the fourth Gospel. In 1977, when we were still serving in Rhodesia, The Officer *magazine – at that time being published each month – accepted from me a series of six articles based on the seven famous 'I am' statements of Jesus. These statements still ring out through all the centuries as implied claims by Our Lord to divine status and hence deserve constant meditative reflection. In 1997 we were appointed to lead the Army's work in the Islamic Republic of Pakistan and during five years in that land were able to build a new Officer Training College. I arranged for seven large marble wall plaques, each carrying one of the seven 'I am' statements in gold lettering, and had these placed prominently around the college campus. Not long after the college opened we received a visit from Colonel Ron Johnson of International Headquarters. On seeing the wall plaques at the college he said simply, 'Every Army college in the world should have these.'*

The Bread of Life

[From The Officer, *July 1977]*

In his profound and beautiful Gospel, the last of the four to be written, John presents seven sayings of Jesus, all of which begin with the phrase, 'I am' (Greek *ego eimi*). This series will attempt to examine each saying (Bread of Life; Light of the World; Door; Good Shepherd; Resurrection and Life; Way, Truth and Life; True Vine) in the context of the discourse in which John has set it.

New Testament Greek offers two ways of saying 'I am'. The shorter and simpler way is to use merely *eimi* – 'I am'. However, for added emphasis the Greek can also say *ego eimi* – literally 'I, I am'. When this stronger formula is used it carries special and additional emphasis and connotes a sense of the phrase being used as a name or title.

The *ego eimi* formula is not original to John but has been borrowed by him, and so its use elsewhere throws light on the meaning it carries in the Gospel. In the Old Testament it is used by the deity as a form of self-disclosure or as a formula of greeting: 'I am the God of your father' (Exodus 3:6); 'I am who I am (Exodus 3:14); 'I am the first and I am the last; besides me there is no god' (Isaiah 44:6).

The same phrase appears in the magical formulae of the ancient Isis cult: 'I am Isis . . . I am creator and created.' It appears also in ancient Greek literature, e.g. in Poimandres where the deity identifies itself with the words, 'I am Poimandres, I am the mind of the Sovereign One'. All these have the Greek *ego eimi* rendering.

Finally, the synoptic Gospels have instances of Jesus stressing his authority by use of a declaratory 'I' (*ego*): 'You have heard that it was said.... But I say unto you ...' (Matthew 5:21,22, plus no fewer than five further examples of the same usage in that chapter).

The examples cited above have this in common, that the 'I am' formula is in some way indicative of the speaker's divine origins and authority. So John's use of the phrase in the seven claims of Jesus amounts to a clear proclamation of Jesus' divine status. Jesus is God. No sensitive reader in those early years could fail to see John's point. Moreover, his use of qualifying adjectives like '*Good* Shepherd', '*True* Vine', '*True* Light', set Jesus apart in no uncertain way from others who falsely claimed to be from God. The claims of Jesus are final, absolute and exclusive, and the symbols of water, bread, light, truth, life, etc., are ideally suited to their purpose, for each is indispensable to human life. Without them we perish.

In John 6:35 we find: 'Jesus said to them, "I am the Bread of Life…".' This claim has to be read in the context of Chapter 6 as a whole, which begins with a description (in verses 5-21) of the feeding of the 5,000 and the walking on the water. John's treatment of the feeding is of special importance as it is the only miracle story to be found in all four Gospels. However, John is alone in linking it with Passover time (see verse 4), inviting the reader to look for some particular theological point here.

The first climax of the narrative comes in verse 15 where the crowd tried 'to make him king'- as if mere mortals could 'make' anything of the One who said, 'I am the Bread of Life'!

The high point of the episode in verses 16-21 is again the theologically loaded 'I am' phrase found in verse 20: 'It is I (*ego eimi*); do not be afraid.' The true significance of the Greek formula is easily lost in the English rendering.

We now reach the discourse itself which starts with verse 26. John's purpose is to draw out the symbolic significance of the preceding narrative. It will be convenient to break the verses into three sections:

(a) Verses 26-34: Here the meaning turns on the contrast between 'food which perishes' and 'food which endures to eternal life' (verse 27). An example of the former is the manna eaten in the wilderness (verse 31). The Jews in the crowd thought that this was rightly called 'bread from heaven' but Jesus quickly discouraged that idea. It would seem that the Jews here wanted Jesus to reproduce the manna miracle in order to substantiate his messianic claim. So Jesus had to explain that although manna fell from the sky, it was not to be regarded as 'the true bread from heaven' (verse 32) which 'gives life to the world' (verse 33).

The new age ushered in by Jesus could not be defined merely 'in terms of crude miracle on the phenomenal level… but in terms of that order of being which is real and eternal' (C.H. Dodd, *The Interpretation of the Fourth Gospel*). However, the people did not understand this and naively asked, 'Lord, give us this bread always.'

(b) Verses 35-50: Their question was answered with Jesus' startling claim, 'I am the Bread of Life'. Rudolf Bultmann (who has been called the supreme interpreter of the 'I am' sayings) explains it in this way: 'Jesus' reply (verse 35), expressed by means of the revelatory formula, *ego eimi*, says that what they are looking for is present in his person' (*The Gospel of John*). He gives living bread and is living bread. God has ordained him to be the divine life-giver and this function is grounded in 'the will of him who sent me' (verse 39) and Jesus' own obedience to that will.

At this point, as in verse 15, the people unwittingly behaved foolishly again by murmuring at Jesus. We murmur at those who are at least our equals. If only they had realised who he (the 'I am') really was! Their difficulty, of course, was that he was, in their eyes, merely 'the son of Joseph' (verse 42). How then could he have originated from heaven? Jesus dealt with this objection very simply in verses 43-50 where he said that recognition of his divine origins and status will be by those who have been 'drawn' or enlightened spiritually by the Father. In verse 48 his original claim is reiterated: 'I am the Bread of Life.' This serves to re-establish the main theme of the discourse.

(c) Verses 51-59: As the section closes, Jesus presses the logical consequences of his claim. If he himself is the Bread of Life and yet gives that bread, it follows that what he gives is none other than himself. Taking this literally, the Jews asked, 'How can this man give us his flesh to eat?' (verse 52). We are reminded of one of Nevil Shute's fictional characters who remarked upon 'the strange ceremony in which Christians eat their god'.

The key to the meaning of eating his flesh lies in verse 56: 'He who eats my flesh and drinks my blood abides in me and I in him' – in other words, mutual indwelling, the Johannine expression for holiness. It is difficult to interpret the mind of the Gospel writer here. Even more difficult is the discovering of what Jesus himself thought in this situation. Most scholars, though by no means all, find in Jesus' words a clear allusion to the eucharist. This view is based on the belief that by the time John was writing, the eucharist was a firmly established ritual.

C.H. Dodd has summarised John's intentions thus: 'The discourse taken as a whole... indicates a progression from false or inadequate conceptions of the messianic status and function of Christ to more adequate conceptions.' In particular, two misconceptions are ruled out: First, Jesus as merely a second Moses (giver of manna). He gives not manna but living bread, and is that living bread. Secondly, Jesus as merely the prophet who is to come and who can be taken to be 'made' a king. Jesus is superior to this. He is in fact *ego eimi*, the One who can by right annex to himself the divine name of 'I am'.

The Light of the World

[From The Officer, *August 1977]*

Matthew, aged four, was peering up at the cloud-filled sky. The Mazowe valley, often bright and sunlit, was on that day sombre and grey, but behind the heavy clouds was the sun and, as if to prove it, a chink of brilliant light shone through a gap in the dark sky. The very dullness of the day accentuated the cheering brilliance of the sun's piercing rays. Matthew pointed upwards and asked, 'Is that where Jesus will come through?'

Even a child of four can recognise instinctively the association of light with Jesus who said, 'I am (*ego eimi*) the Light of the World.'

This astounding claim in John 8:12 has to be seen in the overall context of chapters 7 to 9. It was time for the Feast of Tabernacles, sometimes known as the 'feast of the ingathering' for it was a harvest festival and took its name from the custom of living in tents (tabernacles) during the celebrations. The basic institutions are set out in Leviticus 23:33-43 and Deuteronomy 16:13-15. The Jewish historian, Josephus, described it as 'the holiest and greatest feast among the Hebrews'. Good reason then for Jesus to use this occasion on which to pronounce perhaps the most startling of his *ego eimi* claims (8:12).

John intended the festival allusions to be clear to his readers. Firstly, there is the name of the feast itself Tabernacles. In 1:14 we are told, 'And the Word became flesh and dwelt among us, full of grace and truth.' The translation 'dwelt' is from the Greek *eskenosen* which might equally be rendered 'pitched his tent' or 'tabernacled'. The Jews at the feast did not know it, but God, full of grace and truth, had 'tabernacled' among them. They celebrated the lesser event, ignorant of the greater.

Secondly, part of the festivities consisted of libations (outpourings) from the pool of Siloam which is featured in chapter 9. On the last and greatest day of the feast Jesus stood up and proclaimed as the libations progressed, 'If anyone thirst let him come to me and drink' (7:37). Jesus could offer, not water from a rock, but 'rivers of living water' (7:38). This produced division among them. Furthermore, Siloam means 'Sent' (9:7) but, in John, Jesus himself is 'the Sent One' and is himself a 'river of living water'.

Thirdly, and perhaps most significant of all, were the giant candlesticks burning in the Women's Court of the temple throughout the festivities. They were said to light up every courtyard in the city, so bright was their light. It is against this background that Jesus claims, 'I am the light of the world.' He supersedes the temple rituals and even the Jewish religious calendar. He not only gives light but is 'the Light', revealing hidden things and causing men to judge themselves by their reaction to him. Prime example of this was the Pharisees, who could never bring themselves to admit his claim and retorted, 'You are bearing witness to yourself' (8:14). Their laws required at least two witnesses for a valid testimony and they insisted on applying this human yardstick to the words of the One who was and is *ego eimi*, in fact 'the Word'.

He was the Light: he illuminated and needed no other to illuminate him. Light, by its very nature, witnesses to itself and hence the validity of Jesus' self-witness. Many may need to have their words substantiated by a second witness, but not so with God for he is one and is Truth and cannot lie. He alone knows himself faithfully. The same, therefore, is true of Jesus who is unique, for he alone knows truly his origins and destiny (8:14).

By the beginning of chapter 7, Jesus had already paid two visits to Jerusalem (2:13 and 5:1) and therefore knew well the likely effect of a third visit. Hence he speaks in 7:7 of the world's hatred for him. Even before his appearance at the feast the people were muttering and divided about him (7:11-13).

His brothers, unaware of his true identity, had advised him to go up to the feast and had urged him: '...show yourself to the world' (7:5). They seemed to be suggesting that it might be a tactical error to remain at home when such an opportunity for publicity was available. How shallow! How superficial! How typical of the

55

unenlightened mind! They never dreamt that he was *ego eimi*, the Light of the World, and that for this Light, 'the true light that enlightens every man' (1:9), to be fully revealed prematurely would be disastrous, not for him, but for them, since light is blinding and the unprepared must turn and flee from it.

One of John's key themes in these chapters is the divisive effect of the Light of the World. Light (*phos*) shines and produces division (*schisma*). It is a natural, spiritual law. As if to emphasise the division, the speeches of Jesus in these episodes are continually interrupted and at some points the opponents are even more vocal than Jesus himself. The writer creates a gripping impression of urgency, opposition and conflict.

C.H. Dodd comments, 'The point is further emphasised by repeated statements that Jesus was in danger of his life, and that attempts were made to put him under arrest, or to lynch him on the spot.' In chapters 7 and 8 there are no fewer than 10 statements to this effect. It is no mere accident that the Light of the World discourses are dominated by a motif of conflict. John Marsh has said, 'The more clearly he manifests the Father's glory, the more radical and dangerous is the opposition displayed.'

Jesus was even accused of being demon-possessed (7:20), an echo from the synoptic Beelzebub accusations. Yet not all the crowd agreed and the 'division among the people' (7:43) grew ever deeper. This should be seen on two levels. Superficially, they were divided as to whether or not he was the Christ (Messiah) or a prophet or just another Galilean of whom they could say, 'We know where this man comes from' (7:27). Yet on a much deeper and infinitely more significant level they were divided whether they willed it or not, for Jesus is the Light of the World and his shining presence reveals good and bad alike, that is, those who come to the Light, finding in him a natural place of abode, and those who shun him, unable to face the self-truths so unerringly revealed by him.

We see, therefore, the twin roles played here by *schisma* (division) and *krisis* (judgement). These two themes are interwoven. At the same time it remains true that Jesus came, not to condemn, but to save (3:17). Nevertheless, when the Light appears, 'men inevitably judge themselves by their attitude to it' (C.H. Dodd). It is essentially self-judgement for Jesus judges no one, yet if he does judge, his judgement is true, for it is not he alone that judges, but he and the One who sent him (8:15,16). Thus the Light of the World acts as the catalyst in a process of sifting and selection. Men, through their own response or lack of it, determine for themselves whether they will take up 'the right to become children of God' (1:12).

John, the writer, first articulates the *krisis* theme in 3:19-21. He then makes repeated allusions to it in chapters 7 and 8. In chapter 9, however, where we have the incident of the 'man blind from his birth' (9:1), we discover a direct and explicit treatment of the same theme. The main subject matter in this chapter is not the Light and his divine status, but rather the judging effect (*krisis*) he has upon men.

We have seen the *ego eimi* claim in 8:12. In 9:5 we meet it again: 'I am the Light of the World.' But on this occasion the emphatic *ego eimi* grammatical form is not used. Instead, the place of emphasis is given to the word 'light': 'I am the *Light* of the World' – as contrasted with 8:12 where the emphasis is: '*I am* the Light of the World.'

Chapter 9 is thus to do, not with cosmological status, but with the impact of the Light upon the human race. John communicates this to the reader by using the vehicle of a trial scene. It is all very dramatic, but understandably so for this is judgement (*krisis*) now in action. The blind man is on trial and so is Jesus. The Pharisees purport to judge the Light of the World not knowing that by virtue of his very presence among them they are judging themselves.

John Marsh's treatment of this episode is masterly (see his *Saint John* in the *Pelican New Testament Commentaries*). Jesus heals the man by restoring his sight. Formerly sightless, he now has both sight and insight. Marsh writes, 'The Light of the World had not only shone upon the blind man, but into and through him.' Again Marsh comments, 'Jesus' healing constitutes the re-creation of the whole person, not merely the restoration of one physical function.'

We have to pick up the subtle irony in the question of the onlookers at 9:8 – 'Is not this the man who used to sit and beg?' The true answer should have been, 'No! It is not the same man!' He looked the same, but he was now enlightened in the proper spiritual sense. He answered them, 'I am the man.' John's subtlety is lost in the English rendering. The Greek here at 9:9 says simply, *ego eimi*. This would leap out at an early, Greek-speaking reader as an echo, in human speech, of the divine *ego eimi* name claimed by Jesus. Again Marsh puts it so well: '…some contagion of divinity remains with the healed man…The new disciple 'is found using a term that is, strictly speaking, reserved to his Lord…Yet there is a sense in which the disciple of Jesus can join his Lord and say, "I am" – *ego eimi*.' To enter a true relationship with Jesus, says the Fourth Evangelist, we must abide in him and he in us, hence the not improper echo of the language of the Light of the World.

As the episode develops we meet again the division (*schisma*) engendered by the Light (9:16) and, in their frustration, the Pharisees take it out on the cured man. As yet, his spiritual insight can say only, 'He is a prophet' (9:17). In the end he is driven right back to his famous assertion, '…one thing I know, that though I was blind, now I see' (9:25). This, spoken in awesome ecclesiastical and theological company, stands for ever as a reminder that the believer and his hard-won experience need never cower, even before the most critical and aggressive of audiences.

Nevertheless, they 'cast him out' (9:34) and in so doing they rejected also the Light of the World. Ironically, the cured man had been forced to plead the cause of the Light. He did it unawares, for true realisation was yet to come. Only after a second personal encounter could the man declare, 'Lord, I believe' (9:38). Only then could he worship him with total sight.

In stark contrast, the Pharisees remained ignorant of their true condition. Jesus' final words left them with no doubt. Their refusal to see the true Light was a voluntary acceptance of spiritual blindness. If this had been unavoidable, they might somehow have been excused, but they had chosen their position and had thereby judged themselves.

Door and Good Shepherd

[From The Officer, *September 1977]*

It has been said of John, the Evangelist, that his thought does not move along straight lines. Perhaps nowhere is this demonstrated more clearly than in the Good Shepherd discourse of chapter 10, for here we face what C.K. Barrett describes as 'symbolic discourse in which symbolism and straightforward statement alternate'. Related though they are, the dual images of the Door (*thura*) and the Good Shepherd (*ho poimen ho kalos*) are not directly interchangeable and the latter is further complicated by a double contrasting with (a) thieves and robbers, and (b) hirelings.

Moreover, chapter 10 should not be seen as a self-contained unit but as rounding-off what was begun in chapter 7. The opening device, 'Truly, truly…', is used 25 times in all by John but never to start a new train of thought. It usually indicates a shift in literary form from dialogue to monologue, and this is so here (compare 9:1-41 and 10:1-18).

Before going further, we ought to note the striking likeness between 10:1-18 and Ezekiel 34. The similarities of thought and image are so clear that C.H. Dodd remarks, 'The discourse is not to be fully understood without reference to this passage in the Old Testament which must have been in the author's mind.' Ezekiel sees God's people as a flock of sheep but the rulers of Israel are denounced for being false shepherds who have been more caught up with feeding themselves than feeding the sheep. Further accusations are listed in Ezekiel 34:3-6. The judgement of God is that the false shepherds will be deprived of their privileged positions and God himself will shepherd the flock: '…so will I seek out my sheep; and I will rescue them from all places where they have been scattered… and I will bring them out . . . and I will feed them… I myself will be the shepherd of my sheep' (Ezekiel 34:12-15).

Even a cursory reading of John 10:1-18 reveals its remarkable resemblance to the Old Testament prophecy. Jesus speaks of false and hireling shepherds who neglect their flock, but the Good Shepherd goes before his sheep, defends and rescues them and knows them intimately.

In both passages judgement is pronounced upon the false rulers of God's people. John 10:1-18 condemns those upon whom judgement was passed in 9:41, namely, the Pharisees who, in casting out the man born blind, were effectively scattering the flock which Jesus, the Good Shepherd, will gather (see also 1 Peter 2:25).

We should note, however, one vital difference between the two passages. In Ezekiel 34:23, 24 God resolves the problems of his flock by setting up 'my servant David' as their shepherd. In John, the heroism of the Good Shepherd exceeds anything found in Ezekiel's prophecy, for Christ the Shepherd 'lays down his life for the sheep' (10:11). John is at pains to stress that the death of Jesus is a voluntary self-sacrifice (10:18). John Marsh comments, 'The story of the "passion" in John is not an account of what men did to Jesus, but rather the story of what he did for them.' John 10:18 shows that even when on the Cross, Jesus was actively in full control of the events.

It will be convenient to examine chapter 10 further in three stages:

John 10:1-6

Rudolf Bultmann warns us to resist the temptation to allegorise here. Too much can be read into these verses. The 'sheepfold' and the 'gatekeeper', for example, have no real significance of their own but serve merely as supporting props for the presentation of 'the Shepherd of the sheep' who can be none other than Jesus. Suggestions have been made, however, as to whom the writer means when he mentions 'a thief and a robber'. These are said to 'climb in by another way', attempting entry by illicit means. At best, the passage is obscure and any interpretation has to be tentative. We can note, however, that in 12:6 Judas is labelled a 'thief' and in 18:40 Barabbas is described as a 'robber'. Is it possible that the thieves are those who, like Judas, would try to force the hand of God? Is it also possible that the robbers are men like Barabbas who see armed revolt as the only solution to men's problems?

Whoever they are, these stand in stark contrast to 'the Shepherd of the sheep' who 'enters by the door'. This Shepherd is Jesus. (The discourse is made obscure because here Jesus enters by the door and yet later claims, 'I am (*ego eimi*) the Door' (10:8,9).) We ought to have in mind a picture of several flocks of sheep settled for the night within the courtyard of a house. The setting is urban, not rural. The shepherds would sleep across the courtyard entrance and, next morning, would each call to his own flock. Each flock, recognising its own peculiar call, would respond to its own shepherd who would then lead them out to the fields beyond the village or town. 'The sheep hear his voice, and he calls his own sheep by name and leads them out. When he has brought out all his own, he goes before them, and the sheep follow him, for they know his voice. A stranger ("thief and robber") they will not follow…' (10:3-5).

Those whom the shepherd can call 'his own' have, it would seem, an instinctive, inner security of faith which preserves them from adhering to false or hireling shepherds. Their natural tendency is to obey their master's call. They have been called out from amongst the others and hence are known as a 'called out' community, a church (*ekklesia-* literally: 'called out'). Moreover, they are called individually, 'by name' (10:3). It is the intimacy of the supreme Pastor and 'his own'.

Verse 6 is important. It is one of three key verses (the others are verses 24 and 30) upon which the whole discourse may be said to hang. We are told by the Gospel writer that Jesus used a 'figure' (*paroimia*) with the result that 'they did not understand what he was saying to them'. Almost deliberately, it seems, Jesus veiled his meaning. More than one commentator has seen in the fourth Gospel a 'Messianic secret' parallel to the more generally acknowledged counterpart in Mark. From verse 6 we can jump to verse 24 where the patience of the Jews runs out and they bluntly demand, 'How long will you keep us in suspense? If you are Christ, tell us plainly (*parresia*)'. They get their wish in verse 30 with the clear declaration of Jesus: 'I and the Father are one.' Despite this their reaction to the truth is one of sheer disbelief and horror, 'because you do not belong to my sheep' (10:26).

John 10:7-21

These verses contain two further 'I am' (*ego eimi*) claims of Jesus: 'I am the door of the sheep' (10:8,9) and 'I am the good shepherd' (10:11,14). Christ as the Door is not a frequently mentioned concept, whereas many a preacher and congregation have found inspiration in the image of the Good Shepherd. Marsh says it is 'perhaps the best known and most loved figure of Jesus'.

Nevertheless, the claim, 'I am the Door of the Sheep' has important things to say to us. Most obvious of all is that it establishes in a manner authoritative for Christians what Bultmann terms 'the exclusiveness and absoluteness of the revelation' God makes in Jesus. There is no other satisfactory way to God. Only Jesus is the Door. Only through him can men and women 'go in' for spiritual rest and security, and only through him can they 'go out' and 'find pasture' for their souls. To find such a state of fulfilment we have to yield ourselves unconditionally. Sheep do not strike deals with the shepherd. This is what Bultmann says: 'The security which man finds in the Revealer is not the sort of security which can be bought and bargained for; it can be attained only by giving oneself to him as his own.'

The concept of Christ as 'the Door' speaks to us forcibly also in our capacity as officers of the Army insofar as we exercise a pastoral ministry. Just as the believer can reach God only through Christ the Door, so too we have to approach our work as pastoral agents of God by the same route. We can bring many motives to the influencing of human souls – love of power, satisfaction in controlling others, love of fame and repute, longing to catch the eye of a leader – but all these are 'thief and robber' motives and unworthy of the Christian pastor. William Temple says, 'Nothing can give me warrant for the sacred responsibility of deliberately influencing a soul except that I approach that soul through the door, which is Christ.' (Link this with Mark 10:42-45.)

With the 'Good Shepherd' claim we reach more familiar ground. (For detailed background information on Jesus as Door and as Shepherd the reader should consult C.K. Barrett's *The Gospel According to St John*, pages 308-311.) The Old Testament abounds with descriptions of God as the Shepherd of his people. We have Psalm 23, much loved, quoted and sung; Isaiah 40:11 speaks of God gathering the lambs in his arms and gently leading those that are with young; Ezekiel 34 has been mentioned earlier in this article; and in Zechariah 11:4-9 we find a comparison between false shepherds and God who 'became the shepherd of the flock'.

John's discourse stands in this tradition. The early reader of the Gospel would connect the shepherd with the office of ruler (see above on Ezekiel 34) and then in turn link the Good Shepherd with the divine Ruler. Yet John's use of the Shepherd image goes far beyond that of the Old Testament writers. He sees the Shepherd as literally a 'life and death' figure. The false shepherds identify themselves in that they take the life of the sheep. The Good Shepherd can claim that title precisely because he lays down his life for the sheep. His sacrificial death is not merely incidental to his role as Good Shepherd. It is central and without it there is no role. Moreover, as mentioned earlier, he accepts death voluntarily.

The discourse lays great stress on this: 'For this reason the Father loves me, because I lay down my life that I may take it again. No one takes it from me, but I lay it down of my own accord' (10:17,18). Barrett comments, 'To prove that Jesus accepted death voluntarily was an important point in early Christian apologetic.' This is true, but essentially superficial. John's deeper meaning is articulated by Marsh when he says, 'Where Jesus was most passive (in yielding himself up to death) there he was most active (in bringing eternal life)'. The Good Shepherd's death was not the working of unfeeling fate, but rather the Son's self-offering, the final proof of God's love. We who have entered into the benefits of all this can sing:

> The God of love my shepherd is,
> And he that doth me feed:
> While he is mine and I am his,
> What can I want or need?

John 10:22-39

The scene for the sequel to Jesus' monologue in 10:1-18 is set in Solomon's Porch (10:23) on the outer perimeter of the temple precincts. (See Acts 5:11 which suggests that this was one of the meeting places of the early Christians.) The occasion was one of joyous festivity for it was the Feast of Dedication, celebrating the rededication of the temple in 165 B.C. after Antiochus Epiphanes, the Greek, had desecrated it in a manner especially vile to Jews.

We have already referred to the impatient demand of the Jews for a 'plainly' (10:24) worded answer from Jesus on his Messianic claims. The answer, but not the one they wanted, is given in verse 30: 'I and the Father are one.' This expresses the claim of Jesus in terms of union with God, a theme running right through the Gospel. But further to this we have the 'plainly' worded statements in verses 36 and 38 where the same claim is spoken of in terms of divine sonship – 'I am the Son of God' – and finally in terms of mutual indwelling '…the Father is in me and I am in the Father'. So in fact the Jews' question is answered three times over! It makes no difference, however, for they 'do not belong' (10:26) to Jesus' sheep. Only his sheep hear his voice and follow him, receiving eternal life (10:27,28).

The Jews here share what unbelievers in all ages share – a desire to bring Jesus down to their own level. Thus they accuse him of being a mere man who makes himself God. Ironically, the truth is that God has made himself man! God has 'consecrated' (10:36) Jesus and 'sent (him) into the world'. Again the subtle Johannine sense of the ironic comes through: the Jews are intent upon their own ritual of temple dedication at the Feast, when all the time there stands in their midst the One whom God has 'dedicated' ('consecrated' – set apart for his own purposes) for the salvation of the world.

Unseeing man celebrates the lesser event, ignorant of the greater that is breaking in upon him. Not only this, but the world's notions are so askew that it imagines an attack upon itself to be an attack upon God, and hence the charge of blasphemy in 10:33 and the attempted arrest in 10:39.

At this point the Good Shepherd discourse ends. It is the last 'I am' discourse to be addressed to the people in general. From here on these discourses assume a much more intimate tone. No longer do they talk about the relationship of the Revealer to his own; rather they talk from a basis of that relationship. No longer is it 'they' and 'him', but 'you' and 'I'.

Resurrection and Life
[From The Officer, *October 1977]*

Death is a devastating thing. It seems to us so final, so irreversible, that our minds struggle to take in what Jesus did with the widow's son at Nain (Luke 7:11-17) and the daughter of Jairus (Mark 5:21-43). It could be that the raising of Lazarus (John 11:1-44), because of its seeming impossibility and the place it holds in the Gospels as the supreme miracle of Jesus, has evoked more scepticism than anything else our Lord ever did, and if it were to happen before us today we should hardly be able to believe our eyes.

Thus the Lazarus episode, which John makes the climax of Jesus' earthly ministry and the cause of his execution, presents the reader with the simplest of choices: either believe it or do not. There is nothing amiss in asking ourselves if it could really happen or even if in fact it did happen, but in the end we must give a personal answer. If we can accept Lazarus, we can accept any miracle related in the Gospels, for this is the greatest and most incredible of them all.

To say that it just could not have happened is to tear the heart from the fourth Gospel and indeed, for reasons set out below, from the Christian faith itself. To assent, on the other hand, to the possibility of the miracle is not difficult if we remember that it is not the function of miracles to confirm the divine identity of Jesus. Rather, we should think of Jesus' divine identity as confirming the validity of the miracles.

The scholars say that our best commentary on John 11 is found elsewhere in the Gospel itself. This is at 5:25,28: 'Truly, truly, I say to you, the hour is coming and now is, when the dead will hear the voice of the Son of God, and those who hear will live... the hour is coming when all who are in the tombs will hear his voice and come forth....' The raising of Lazarus fulfils these words. Lazarus was in the tomb (11:17), Jesus called with a loud voice (11:43) and the dead man came out (11:44).

Before we analyse the 'I am' (*ego eimi*) claim of Jesus in 11:25, it is worth noting the strangely divergent treatment this chapter has received at the hands of the commentators. Some manage to discover all manner of inconsistencies in the narrative, so much so that they almost despair of finding any meaning in it. Others, more happily, see the raising of Lazarus as a simple story with a simple, albeit profound, message.

Professor C.F.D. Moule is in the former group. Writing in *Theology* journal (March 1975), he confesses a staunch belief in the hereafter, a belief which sustained him through the premature loss of a dearly loved brother. ('Lord, if you had been here, my brother would not have died.') Yet he finds Lazarus 'a difficult story', 'positively confusing' and 'bristling with questions'. Why should Lazarus have been deliberately allowed to die and then restored to life? What is the message for the reader from the restoration of a merely physical life? How can the mere re-animation of Lazarus say anything to us about that ultimate life hereafter? Was Lazarus a man of faith? Why are we not told of his attitude to Jesus? Why the deliberate and apparently artificial delay when Jesus heard the news of Lazarus being ill? Why did Jesus purposely allow a grievous situation to develop merely in order to reverse it? Moule asks all this and more and can only conclude that John 11 is 'the most effective way' of teaching me that the meaning of life is not a bit simple nor clear'.

In contrast, most of us would find C.K. Barrett much more helpful. He says that the meaning of John 11 is as simple as the narrative itself. Jesus, in his obedience to and dependence upon the Father (see the prayer in verses 41 and 42), has the authority to give life to whom he will. He is the Resurrection (*anastasis*) and the Life (*zoe*). Therefore, apart from him, there is no resurrection and no life. Where he is, resurrection and life must be. This, in a nutshell, is what chapter 11 is all about.

Nevertheless, Moule's questions are legitimate. Space permits us to comment here only upon the puzzling delay by Jesus mentioned in 11:6. Firstly, it appears that Jesus waited so that Lazarus was well and truly dead. This may sound strange, but the Jewish belief was that beyond the third day in the grave a total dissolution of life took place and the soul left the body. So, in the case of Lazarus who was *tetartaios* (11:39) – literally 'a four-dayer' – there was no chance at all of someone later suggesting that he had not truly died in the first place. Secondly, and perhaps more importantly, do we need to seek at all for explanations of Jesus' behaviour here? I recall the words of a respected Army officer: 'God's clocks are never wrong.' Just so, the work of Jesus has its own hour and no man could pressurise the 'I am' into action not in harmony with divine timing.

We come now to a closer look at 11:25, where Jesus claims, 'I am (*ego eimi*) the Resurrection and the Life; he who believes in me, though he die, yet shall he live, and whoever lives and believes in me shall never die.'

The concept of 'life' in John is difficult to pin down. Rudolph Bultmann rightly tells us that it is not to be defined or described. It is something so completely the gift of God that it can only be hinted at by human language. Yet we have to attempt an understanding of how the Evangelist uses the word. He tells us that it comes as a gift from the Spirit and that Jesus' words are 'spirit and life' (6:63). The disciples openly confess this at 6:68; and at 20:31 John says that those who believe that Jesus is the Christ have life in his name. Altogether, the term 'life' is used 36 times by John in his Gospel. The verb 'to live' is found 16 times and the derivative 'to give life', three times. Frequently we find the phrase 'eternal life' (*zoe aionios*) but there is no real difference between 'life' and 'eternal life' in the mind of the writer. For him the terms are interchangeable.

The Johannine concept of life is principally eschatological, referring to a future life in an age yet to come. In 11:25, our key verse, we can discern two different but complementary aspects of this. There is life for those who have died ('I am the Resurrection') and also for those who 'shall never die' ('I am the Life'). In other words, the two concepts of (a) resurrection and (b) life should be seen as corresponding to the two clauses which make up the rest of verses 25 and 26.

What is especially striking is the idea that 'whoever lives... shall never die'. The resurrection of which Jesus spoke is something which may take place before bodily death and has as its result the possession of eternal life here and now. Naturally enough, Moule's question springs to mind as to what the bodily resurrection of Lazarus has to do with eternal life either here or hereafter.

Quite simply, we must regard the physical reconstruction of Lazarus as but a symbol of the life that is true and ultimate life in Jesus. The raising in John 11 is not the same in kind as that of believers in the afterlife. The former is only a sign of the latter. The main point to be grasped is that if Jesus' words (and note that here bare words produce bodily life) have such power here and now, then how much more power will they carry hereafter.

For the believer, John 11 means that the hereafter can break into the present and hence the significance of the third title spoken by Martha in verse 26: 'He who is coming into the world'. Jesus is the Eternal invading the realms of Time, but eternal life in Jesus is both now and later. Look at 6:54 where this paradox is clearly stated: 'He who eats my flesh and drinks my blood has eternal life, and I will raise him up at the last day.' Present and future interact here, so that it would be an error to suppose that death alone is the gateway to true life in Jesus. The fourth Gospel leaves us in no doubt that present enjoyment of eternal life is for the believer: 3:36; 5:24; 6:47; 6:54. The believer has eternal life now, in the midst of this life.

Consequently, we may Christianise the words of Philo of Alexandria (20 BC - AD 40): 'Today is boundless and inexhaustible eternity. Months, years and time are notions of men. The true name of eternity is Today. '

It was stated earlier that denial of the raising of Lazarus could be seen as a denial of something central to the Christian faith, for at the heart of Christianity lies a firm belief in resurrection. Jesus said, 'I am the Resurrection....' For this reason, together with faith in the resurrection underlying every sermon in Acts and every book in the New Testament, we have to recognise that without its bold assertion of resurrection, Christianity falls apart (see the words of Paul in 1 Corinthians 15). Indeed, resurrection has to be the very starting-point for any thinking about the Christian religion. A.M. Ramsey, speaking of resurrection, calls it 'a doctrine which sums up the genius of the Christian faith'.

We have to preach and teach it, and not just on Easter Sunday. We have to overcome those all too simplistic ideas which equate the resurrection of Jesus, or our resurrection hereafter, with what happened to Lazarus. Resurrection is not resuscitation or mere physical reconstruction. Yet we can continue to speak intelligibly of the resurrection of the body (see our 11th Article of Faith) because we need not limit the word 'body' to merely the body as we know it in this earthly state. In the resurrection hereafter, to borrow Ramsey's words once more, 'there will not be the solidity of the flesh, the liquid blood, the sinews, the structure of the limbs; yet the body will be there'. Moreover, the body's form will be determined by the spiritual conditions of that existence to come (1 Corinthians 15:35-44).

So let us present to our people, and to those beyond our ranks, the question Jesus asked of Martha: 'Do you believe this?' (John 11:27). With the question unasked, how can we expect to hear the all-decisive 'Yes, Lord'?

Way, Truth and Life

[From The Officer, *November 1977]*

How often have we heard it said that John's Gospel is 'too deep for me'? Part of the key to this book may lie in understanding the 'misunderstandings' used by John as a literary device to advance his argument. There are four clear examples of this in the passage now under consideration: the questions of Simon Peter (13:36,37), Thomas (14:5), Philip (14:8) and Judas (14:22). If we try to get inside and unravel each of these, we may thereby come closer to an understanding of Jesus and his claims.

Simon Peter (13:31-14:4)
The section opens with Jesus predicting his imminent death. The disciples are told that time is now running out and furthermore they will not be able to follow where Jesus is going. There is then given the 'new command' – that they should love one another with the love he has offered them. Commenting on this love, John Marsh says, 'In a word, it is to be love of the kind that will "reverse the roles", and bring the leader to serve as a slave, the innocent to serve as the guilty, in the love that will bring peace to the world by its sacrificial quality.'

All this is too much for Peter whose mind is still on the impending departure of his Lord and so he demands, 'Lord, where are you going?' Practical Peter, still thinking on the mundane level of this world, has failed to realise that the departure of Jesus is not an event taking place within the human sphere at all. It is not a human undertaking, but one that lies outside the limited dimensions of ordinary mortals. Jesus' departure is both a departure from the world and a victory over the world. To think of it as just another journey is simply foolish, and so Peter's understanding has progressed little further than that of the Jews in 7:35 and 8:32.

If the departure of Jesus is of this kind, the kind that transcends human dimensions, so too is the 'following' of his disciples, for discipleship involves taking on the attributes, in one's nature and actions, of the One called Master. Here Peter is again sadly astray. In verse 37, heroically he declares, 'I will lay down my life for you.' Peter has heard the 'I am' claims of Jesus, has listened to his teaching, has witnessed the miracles and still he thinks he can act for the Revealer. It is the Revealer who has entered human life for Peter. It is the Revealer who will shortly die for him. Before this man could truly follow, that is, follow out of faith and not out of sheer human heroism, he had to be brought low. Only after the crushing words of verse 38 had come true could Peter's discipleship be based on something other than the physical courage inherent in his personality. As Bultmann puts it, all that Jesus wanted of Peter was an 'expectant preparedness', one that would equip him for the return of Jesus as the 'Spirit of Truth'. That was all that was expected of Peter, and that is all that is expected of us.

Chapter 14 opens with explicitly comforting words. The disciples had taken a series of terrible blows: they had learned that Jesus was about to die, that a traitor was present in their midst, and that Peter, of all people, would prove disloyal. Against this background Jesus offers words of comfort, but words of exhortation too: 'Believe in God, believe also in me.' He urges them not to abandon faith in him merely because events, to human eyes, are taking a turn for the worse. In fact, to abandon faith in Jesus would be to abandon faith also in God, for faith in God is mediated only by Jesus who claimed: 'I am the way… no one comes to the Father, but by me.'

Thomas (14:5-7)

As with Peter, Thomas's misapprehension serves to bring out deeper truth. Not unnaturally, Thomas differentiates between route and destination, means and end. However, these are categories of human thought and they can have no application to the work and person of the 'I am'. Defying the logic of men, Jesus claims to be, at one and the same time, Revealer and Revealed, both Means and End.

'I am the way, and the truth, and the life,' he answers Thomas. As in the other *ego eimi* claims the emphasis is on the personal

73

pronoun: 'I am the way ... (For 'life' in John see article four in this series.) We should note that 'way' (*hodos*) was a term used by early believers to denote the Christian faith: see Acts 9:2; 22:4; 24:14. The first readers of John would have picked up this allusion instantly. The Gospel writer conceives of Jesus as the means of access to God and, moreover, the sole and exclusive means of access. (Link this with the concept of Jesus as 'the Door'-10:8.) If in his own person and being Jesus embodies the Way to God, it follows that he does not need a 'way' for himself. His access is direct; ours is indirect and mediated through him.

Bultmann warns us against thinking of Jesus as mediating access to God and then becoming in some sense superfluous. Rather, he is the Way in such a manner as to be at the same time the Goal or Destination, for he is also, as the claim in 14:6 reveals, Truth and Life. The normal rules of human logic fall away here, feeble and inadequate. This is the supreme instance when truth and logic are not to be thought synonymous.

The exclusiveness of Jesus' claim here should be squarely faced. John lines up with the writer of Acts who says of Jesus: 'There is salvation in no one else, for there is no other name under heaven given among men by which we must be saved' (Acts 4:12). If the claims of Jesus are exclusive, so too must be the claims of those who love and serve him. It is always tempting, especially in a missionary setting (from which I write), to be ever so tolerant of other faiths. If tolerance means respect, that is fine, but if it has to mean watering down our own beliefs almost to the point of syncretism, then count this writer amongst the intolerant. Every man deserves to hear the truth and to be introduced to the One who is Truth. (I speak here only of the contents of our message and not of methods.) To offer the Moslem, the Hindu, the Buddhist or the ancestral spirit worshipper a Christianity any less exclusive and absolute in its claims than the claims of its Founder is paternalism at its worst, for it takes what a man needs most, namely the gospel of Jesus, and having diluted it, offers it as the genuine article. Dr William Hendriksen, commenting on 14:6 states, 'With Christ removed there can be no redemptive truth, no everlasting life; hence, no way to the Father.' If we dilute the gospel for fear of giving offence, we do men a disservice and fail in our calling.

The absoluteness of the Christian faith is further impressed by John upon his readers in Jesus' words: 'I am…the truth.' Jesus is the truth; he does not simply state it. Christian truth is not a set of proposals to be understood, learned, preserved and handed on like mere doctrines. In its highest and purest form Christian truth is Jesus. Therefore this Truth is to be met, encountered, loved and obeyed. The test of a true believer is not whether he knows the truth, but whether he is of the Truth. For the Truth is a person. Pilate got it wrong when he asked, 'What is truth?' (18:38), for he should have said, 'Who is Truth?'

In the fourth Gospel 'truth' means knowledge of absolute and ultimate reality. It is the opposite of 'flesh', 'world' and 'devil' for it is of the Spirit (16:13) and Jesus himself will return as the 'Spirit of truth' (14:17). Truth saves and liberates (8:32), is spoken by (8:45) and revealed in (14:6) Jesus, and the disciples are to be sanctified 'in the truth' (17:17,19). At the outset of the Gospel, Jesus is said to be 'full of grace and truth' (1:14). In him therefore is absolute reality; and life apart from Jesus is a counterfeit, a sham and a pretence.

Philip (14:8-14)

'Philip said to him, "Lord, show us the Father, and we shall be satisfied".' Like Peter and Thomas before him, Philip just did not understand. Despite all that Jesus had said, he still thought he could have a direct revelation of God. In this he attempted, unwittingly, to place himself on the level of Jesus, for only Jesus has direct access to the Father. Philip's question, for two reasons, was an unintended snub to his Lord. Firstly, the question denied the effectiveness of Jesus' role as Revealer. Philip failed to see that his fellowship (and ours) with Jesus would lose all significance unless he were acknowledged as the One whose sole mission is to reveal God.

Demanding a direct revelation implies that the indirect revelation offered in Jesus is not enough. Secondly, to demand that Jesus should show them the Father is to assume that the Father is in fact other than the Son. This explains why Jesus' reply to Philip in verses 9-11 is couched in terms relative to the oneness, the unity of the Father and himself. It is a mistake to suppose there is knowledge of the Father to be had beyond Jesus himself. The Evangelist's point is clear – just as there is no access to God without Jesus, neither is there knowledge of God without him.

Next Jesus tells the disciples that they will do 'greater works' than he has done. These will be accomplished in his 'name', but not by uttering 'Jesus' like some magical incantation. Underlying this verse is the Old Testament concept of a name summarising the personality. Hence, the 'greater works' (taken by the best commentators to mean the winning of souls) will be achieved simply because the person (and personality) of Jesus is indwelling the believers through the mediation of the Spirit. In this way, the 'greater works' are in fact still the works of Jesus, without whom we can do nothing (15:5).

Judas (14:15-24)
The question posed by Judas, coming in the middle of these verses dealing with the return of Jesus, is described by Marsh as 'the question of all disciples in all ages'. Why not some final, all-decisive proof of God to convince once and for all even the most stubborn of unbelievers? 'Why not manifest yourself to the world, O God?'

In short, God has chosen his own distinctive method of revealing himself to men and it is this method of which Jesus speaks in verses 15-24. The Paraclete (Counsellor, Helper, Advocate) will come to the believers. He will be for them what Jesus had been, except not visible to the eye. He will be discernible to faith and faith alone (14:17).

It is clear that John intends us to understand that the Spirit is none other than Jesus himself: 'I will come again' (14:3); 'I will come to you' (14:18); 'You will see Me' (14:19); 'I will…manifest Myself'

(14:21); 'We will come...' (14:23). The advent of the Spirit is foretold in verses 15-17 and 25-27. Between these sections the dominant theme is the return of Jesus. It follows that the advent of the Spirit and the return of Jesus are one and the same event. For the writer of this Gospel it could be that the primitive Christian ideas of Pentecost and Parousia (Second Coming) have been fused into one. Moreover, the unique Johannine teaching on the role and work of the Spirit must ever be kept before us to check and balance any tendency to overstress the Pauline concept of the Holy Spirit, spotlighted as it is these days by some 'charismatic' Christians. A truly scriptural understanding of the Holy Spirit must pay adequate attention to the views of John as well as to those of Paul who writes at length about the supernatural gifts of the Spirit.

Whilst Paul wrote out of the ferment of primitive Christianity, John can offer us a calm reappraisal, a reinterpretation of those early events as seen from a vantage point later in time. True to the gospel tradition, he has nevertheless restructured the early events, discarding much of the primitive conceptual framework and introducing for our lasting benefit a Gospel rich in mystical spirituality.

The True Vine

[From The Officer, *December 1977]*

We have come to the seventh and last of the great 'I am' sayings of John's Gospel: 'I am the vine, the genuine one.' Even the lapse of 20 centuries cannot dim the poignancy of Jesus' words for the little band of loyal followers at that fateful moment. Loyal, yes, for Judas had left to do what had to be done and the 'embryo church', as John Marsh calls it, was left alone to hear uttered the spiritual mysteries of the True Vine and the branches. They must have been nervous, dependent men, hoping that somehow their fears of impending separation from him were ill-founded. So he met their dependence and eased their fears by speaking to them of unbreakable union with himself, of mutual indwelling – he with them and they with one another.

The words we find in John 15:1-17 are words of intimacy. Forming part of the longest monologue in the fourth Gospel, they are about the relation of the disciples to their risen Lord and to one another. To complement this, 15:18-16:11 turns outward to look at the relation of the disciples to a hostile world, but our attention must focus on the first 17 verses with their dominant, daring theme of union with God.

The Gospel writer is too skilled a craftsman to thrust this concept upon his reader without due preparation, and so, by the time chapter 15 is reached the mind has met and received such statements as: 'He who eats my flesh and drinks my blood abides in me, and I in him' (6:56); and 'I and the Father are one' (10:29); and 'You will know that I am in my Father, and you in me, and I in you' (14:20). John's Gospel may rightly be described as the 'Gospel of Unity', for this idea of mystical oneness recurs again and again, reaching a climax in chapter 15 and again in chapter 17 where Jesus prays 'that they might be one'. The message is clear enough. Without the Father, the Son can do nothing. Without the Son, we who are believers are similarly helpless. To rescue us from our helplessness, the unity of

Father and Son is reproduced in the unity of the risen Christ and the believer. As the Father performs his works in the Son, so does the Son perform his works in the believer.

If Paul were asked to express the same concept he would talk about being 'in Christ'. John elects to use the imagery of the vine: 'I am the true vine... you are the branches... apart from me you can do nothing... abide in my love.' What a startling concept! We who are mortals are grafted to the True Vine and thereby share directly in the life that is his! But most of us have no first-hand experience of vines and so some of the impact of the symbolism may escape us. The first readers of John 15 would have come to this picture of Christ, the True Vine, as inhabitants of a vine-growing country but, infinitely more significant, as people accustomed to thinking symbolically in terms of vines and viticulture when it came to matters of religion.

References to God's chosen people, Israel, as being God's 'vine' are common in the Old Testament: Isaiah 5, Jeremiah 2 and 12, Ezekiel 15 and 19, Hosea 10. All these, however, reveal Israel as a failed, degenerate vine. In contrast we have Psalm 80:8-17 where the writer pleads for a restoration of the vine: 'Turn again, 0 God of hosts! Look down from heaven and see; have regard for this vine, the stock which thy right hand planted.' The passage goes on to mention 'the man of thy right hand' and 'the son of man'. These phrases should be taken as references to the king of that day, but 'son of man' echoes the famous passage in Daniel 7 and would inevitably come to mind upon reading John 15 because of the coupling of 'son of man' and 'vine' in Psalm 80.

John has taken it all a step further and has made explicit in his Gospel what hitherto had been only potentially coherent strands of thought. The Son of Man has come and has claimed for himself, as an individual, a description formerly used only of a community, Israel. However, Israel is the failed and fruitless vine and has been superseded by Christ, the True Vine. In comparison with him, all other claims to being the 'vine' of God are false.

John may even have been attempting a polemical point here against the synoptic writers, for in the first three Gospels there is evidence (not proof) that the disciples considered themselves to have become the 'new Israel' (Matthew 19:28, Mark 10:37 and Luke 22:30). John cannot endorse this line of thought. The 'new Israel', the 'true Israel', is not a community, not even the chosen disciples; it is none other than Jesus himself. What might once have been embodied in a nation is now embodied in the person of the risen Christ so that he alone can claim: 'I am (*ego eimi*) the true vine.'

After this initial declaratory statement in verse 1, the judicial role of God the Father is explained. Fruitless branches are lopped off altogether and even those which produce must be pruned. This may be painful but since it results in added fruitfulness should be welcomed in the life of the believer. As steel has been tempered, as gold refined, so Christian usefulness presupposes the pruning touch of God. Our function, our duty, is to bear fruit, in fact to bear 'more fruit'. We are not pruned to enjoy peace and prosperity or to wallow in past successes. We are pruned to bear more fruit, and so there can be no backward glance, no resting on our laurels. None of us can rely on what we have already achieved for there is 'no discharge in this war'. Bultmann says that God 'continually demands something new from us'. We should take it as a mark of confidence.

Pruning and purging go together. Merely by being open to the words of Jesus we are cleansed and fitted for fruit-bearing (15:3). His words, his sayings bring purity to our lives as we let them invade and overtake us. So whence purity? By systems, activities, doctrines, status, promotion? No, simply by the words of Jesus.

Abiding in Christ (15:4) is both an active and passive thing. Actively it means obedience to his commands (15:10); passively it is not a holding on by us but rather a willingness to be held by him. In chapter 6 he revealed himself as Living Bread, the Sustainer of life. Here in chapter 15 he shows himself to be the Vine, the Origin and Source of life. That is why 1:3 says that 'without him was not anything made that was made' – apart from him, nothing; with him, infinite possibilities. Hence the injunction: 'Abide in me, and I in you', words which to William Temple 'gather up the whole meaning of what it is to be a Christian'. No branch can bear fruit by itself and so all Christian worship, discipline, planning, evangelistic effort must derive from a simple 'abiding'. If it does so derive, it is good. If it does not, it is bad.

The question arises naturally as to what constitutes 'fruitbearing'. Marsh says: 'To bear fruit is not simply to have one's evangelical efforts succeed; it is to be with the Lord in witness, both in word and deed, in action and in passion, in suffering and in joy, in defeat and victory, in death and resurrection.' So let us avoid too narrow a concept of what it is to be a fruitful Christian.

Seekers are one sort of fruit. There are many others. An empty mercy seat is a sad and disappointing thing which can and does grieve an officer's heart, but it is not an infallible sign of failure. This writer has taken to heart the advice of one older and wiser: 'Preach each time as if it were your last, and God will take care of the question of seekers.' In the final analysis it is his work anyway, not ours. Happily, God's notion of fruitfulness is much wider than our own at times. That being so, let us take stock and take heart!

Verse 7 suggests that the fruit of sanctified praying will flow from a mutual abiding of the believer in Christ and Christ's words in the believer. Here the Greek *hremata* (words) means specific sayings of Jesus as over against his teaching in general which would be *logoi* as in verse 3. If Jesus' sayings abide in us, then Truth abides for his words are truth (18:37) and he is the Truth (14:6). Moreover, since believers are of the truth they will receive the ministrations of the Spirit of Truth (16:13-15) who will interpret ever afresh the words of the Master.

The promise given here is awesome: 'Ask whatever you will, and it shall be done for you.' God help us if we ever treat this as if it were some magical incantation or a licence for irresponsible petitionary prayer! What we frequently overlook is the precondition in the first half of the verse: 'If you abide in me....' Is it really possible then to

81

reach that stage of growth where we are incapable of asking anything contrary to the will of God? Yes, it is. God's word does not toy with us by demanding the impossible and we Salvationists, who teach and preach the life of holiness, are called to witness unceasingly to the possibility of such spiritual heights. Mutual indwelling, writes William Temple, 'so purifies the heart that at last there is no need for any deliberate control of desire, because desire itself is sanctified'.

The injunction to abide is reiterated in verse 9 but this time it is: 'Abide in my love.' There is no difference in meaning from 'abide in me' but such abiding, as Bultmann reminds us, is not a self-sufficient wallowing in the fact of our salvation or mere indulgence in devotions. It is keeping the commandments of Christ, for verse 10 goes on to say: 'If you keep my commandments you will abide in my love….' Love and obedience therefore are counterparts, mutually dependent, each giving rise to the other. Moreover, the obedience offered by the believer to Christ is to be a parallel to that offered by Christ to the Father (15:10). What is already reality in him is to become reality in us, but there are yet further implications. The vertical relationship between the believer and his Lord must be worked out in horizontal relationships between believer and believer. Verse 10 has shown that to stay in Jesus' love I must obey his command and now verse 12 tells me that the command is: 'Love one another as I have loved you.' Therefore, if I want to stay in his love, I must love you, my fellow Christian, and his love for me is to be the model for my love for you.

Those who are obedient are given the status of 'friend' of Christ. Although he is 'Master' and although the natural correlative would be to call us 'slaves', we are treated as 'friends' (15:14). We are free persons for we know the truth and have thereby been set free (8:32). It is obedience and knowledge which distinguish a friend from a slave in this context, but verse 16 reminds us that friendship with Christ, whilst involving reciprocity of a kind, is not built upon equality. That is not possible in a relationship with Jesus. The initiative is always his, for we are subject to his 'choosing' and to his 'appointing', the appropriate response on our part being a vital faith and an ongoing willingness to be fruit-bearing.

The section closes with yet again the command to love one another. Whilst the emphasis is on love between Christians, love for the unbeliever is not precluded. God's love is for all mankind (1:29 and 3:16), but in chapter 15 the main concern is the binding together of believers into a oneness that will make for maximum effectiveness. That oneness is the unity of branches which are all equally dependent upon Christ, the True Vine.

CHAPTER 6

Insights in Modern Fiction – Morris West

[At the end of 1978 we completed our term of service in Rhodesia and returned to London where we enjoyed Christmas with loved ones. Colonel Victor Keanie, at that time Chief Secretary to the Chief of the Staff, interviewed us in his office at International Headquarters (IHQ). He was kindly and gracious. We learned that the Army would like us to choose between serving next in a corps appointment at Enfield in North London or my being made a member of the IHQ Literary Department. The latter would have left Helen without an appointment of her own, something commonly accepted in those days. Also I had a strong sense that if I were to go on writing for the Army it should be out of a setting that kept me close to the action and the front line. So we went to the Enfield Citadel Corps were we spent three and a half happy and fruitful years. In 1979 The Officer *magazine carried a series entitled* Insights in Modern Fiction. *I was pleased to be asked to contribute a short piece and did so featuring the novelist Morris West, this appearing in September 1979.]*

In the last 20 years Morris West has written a score of novels but it was *The Devil's Advocate* published in 1959 that took him into the best-seller lists. It sold more than six million copies and was made into both a play and a film. In 1963 there followed *The Shoes of the Fisherman*, another best-seller also made into a film by

MGM. Both books hinge on religious themes and make for compelling reading.

West was born in Australia in 1916 and his first job after university was teaching in schools belonging to the Catholic order of the Christian Brothers. So it is that the two works of fiction mentioned here have to do with the Roman Catholic Church. *The Shoes of the Fisherman* describes the election of a young and non-Italian pope from a communist country. (What Morris West imagined in 1963 came true in 1978!) Kiril Lakota, the hero of the book, having spent 17 years in Siberian prison camps, attends his first papal conclave in Rome only to find himself elected to that elevated and onerous office. We share in his emotions of the moment, his fears and misgivings, his dreadful sense of inadequacy and his desperate waiting upon God for strength and wisdom.

We accompany him upon an incognito excursion into the streets of Rome where he rediscovers the pain and starkness of life as it is lived by the ordinary and poverty-stricken. He re-encounters death in the slums and later that night records his reactions: 'I am troubled tonight. I am solitary and perplexed. I have seen men die, but the sad and solitary exit which I witnessed tonight in a Roman tenement afflicts me strangely. The words of the woman who saw it with me still ring in my ears – "They can cope with death. It's the living that defeats them." It seems to me that this defeat is the measure of our failure in the ministry of the Word.'

He wrestles, too, with pressing moral issues when only a stone's throw from the Vatican comes a series of deformed births due to an incompletely tested birth control drug. He learns of the young doctor who ensures that no such baby survives and he recalls his own dilemma in Siberia when nursing a friend dying in agony: 'It's a terrible thing to see so much suffering. It degrades and terrifies those who see it but cannot alleviate it. That's why I understand but cannot condone what the doctor did. It seems almost as though one would be bestowing a divine mercy with the gift of death. But one is not divine, one cannot dispense either life or death.'

To an extraordinary extent the Army officer reading these novels can identify with the leading ecclesiastical characters – their search for God, their burden of responsibility, for the people and their constant awareness of being but mortal. We can share, too, in their ideals. Before Kiril is elected, one American cardinal thinks aloud about the man they need from God to lead them: 'A man for the people and of the people. A man who could bleed for them, and scold them, and have them know all the time that he loved them.' This could have been said at any High Council or for that matter at any candidates' selection board for these are the very qualities which have made us what we are by the grace of God and which have won for the Army the respect and affection of the world.

Then again, the new pope's words to his cardinals could have been Booth's to his officers: 'We are what we are, for the service of God through the service of man. If we lose contact with suffering, sinful, lost, confused men crying in the night, women agonising, children weeping then we too are lost because we shall be negligent shepherds who have done everything but the one thing necessary.' Later in the novel the same 'Salvationist' ring is there again: 'I believe there is only one way into the future. We take the truth like a lamp and we walk out like the first apostles and tell the good tidings to whoever will listen. If history stands in our way we ignore it. If systems inhibit us we dispense with them. If dignities weigh us down we cast them aside…. Find me men with fire in their hearts and wings on their feet. Send them to me and I will send them out to bring love to the loveless….'

Although not in orders himself, Morris West has grasped in a remarkable way the issues facing ministers of the gospel today. Recently he spoke of these on BBC radio and witnessed to his own standing as a Christian. He sees as not the least of today's problems the communication gap between people and Church. How does one present the gospel to modern man? In *The Devil's Advocate* we meet Blaise Meredith, an English priest destined to die within the year from cancer and whose last assignment is to act as devil's advocate, an official papal office, in the claims to sainthood made for the martyred Giancomo Nerone by the people of his village in Italy. Meredith's life has been spent in the confines of Vatican offices and libraries. Now at the end of his days he is thrust without warning among peasant people living simply from the land. It is his duty to subject the life of their deceased hero to the minutest analysis before any claim to sainthood can be taken further. Inevitably he finds he is out of touch both as man and priest. He complains to a colleague of 'the difficulty of accurate communication between the clergy and the laity'. He admits to teaching 'a truth we claim to be essential to man's salvation' but at the same time talking to the people every Sunday with words that fail to reach them. Before he can resolve this for himself he runs out of time, but we who also preach and teach every Sunday share the same plight and fight the same battles from the platform. Somehow we have to speak the language of God in the language of the people and since the people's language refuses to be static the task is never over.

West raises the same issue in *The Shoes of the Fisherman* but this time is more positive: 'The best one could hope was that, here and there, the Word would take fire in the soul of a man, would brighten his eyes with vision and set him striding out to achieve a divine impossible… there was no other choice but to go on preaching, teaching, urging to action and to wait, empty of all but hope, on the promise of the Holy Spirit.'

Officer or priest, we can identify with that.

CHAPTER 7

At the Frontiers of Ethics

Toward the conclusion of our officer service in Rhodesia I submitted to The Officer *magazine for publication a short series of three articles on Christian social ethics dealing with: pornography (an evil that is still the scourge of many today including not a few in religious circles); punishment and forgiveness (matters that arise constantly in the field of criminal justice and penology); disobedience to the state (civil disobedience and the concept of the 'just revolution') and these were published in July - October 1978 under the series title of* More Aspects of Christian Ethics, *building on the short studies which appear in chapter 2 of this book.. Space does not permit the reproduction of these three articles in this volume. Later, when serving as the Legal and Parliamentary Secretary at International Headquarters in London, it proved possible to write a further series on ethical issues,* At the Frontiers of Ethics, *which appeared in January - June 1983. This series (covering issues of biological ethics, nuclear warfare, and sexuality) is reproduced here as chapter 7. As with the earlier chapter on ethical issues I have intentionally sought not to update the technical content or topical references in order to allow the ongoing relevance of the central ethical issues to stand out. Readers will note carefully that legal references cannot be assumed still to be applicable today.*

Introducing the Issues

In the months to come, a further five articles will appear in this series. Two will discuss artificial insemination; two will look at nuclear warfare and the last will deal with homosexuality. At first, the reader may think this is a fairly random selection of topics, but what links them is the fact that in none of these areas of ethical debate do we have a settled and agreed Christian point of view.

Artificial insemination is making its impact on our world through advancing scientific capabilities. New techniques are perfected with almost breathtaking regularity and we are left with a novel practice in our midst without having had time or opportunity to think through the moral implications of its use.

Nuclear weapons, it seems, have been around much longer and the moral debate has ebbed and flowed for at least a generation, but nuclear science is never static. New weapons come along, refinements are introduced, military options change and political probabilities grow less certain. In this area too, Christians have failed to agree on the ethics.

Homosexuality may seem a far cry from nuclear warfare, but it also is a topic of current debate and some long-settled Christian attitudes have recently been shaken.

This series, then, is an attempt to survey the facts and the ethical discussion as it now stands in relation to these three issues. It may be necessary to conclude that no satisfactory moral stance has yet been achieved in a given area, or we may end up reaffirming old attitudes despite new data. Essentially, we shall find ourselves frequently on terrain still to be properly charted by modern ethicists. The data has outstripped us, the techniques have raced ahead of us, and we are left struggling to formulate adequate Christian responses to new possibilities, indeed to new actualities. In short, we are at the frontiers of ethics, in territory as yet unexplored or for which the long-trusted charts have been challenged and cast aside.

Artificial insemination

The artificial insemination of women with the seed of male donors (AID) is a practice now widely established on an international scale. For those who are unable to have children 'naturally' it may at first seem an ideal solution. Here is a technique not involving adultery which may produce a child, and many, though by no means all, family doctors are willing to recommend that the pain of childlessness be eased in this way. Yet couples should be encouraged to pause and weigh up intelligently all that is involved. Should any means be used to solve the problem? Is this particular means morally acceptable? Is the donor's action moral? What of the child that may be born? Whose will it be? Will the husband later regret having opted for AID? Will he later resent the child? Is AID akin to marital infidelity? Are the doctors acting ethically? What controls are there in the selection of donors or of recipient wives?

These questions cannot even begin to be answered without some knowledge of the medical facts involved. Then the psychological factors too must be weighed before judging the entire matter in the light of Christian, scriptural insights. Only then can we begin to see whether the intended action might infringe the rights of others and whether or not the technique is dehumanising.

Nuclear weapons

If AID raised questions of individual morality for married couples and others involved in the process, nuclear weapons raise moral issues relevant to every human being on the face of our planet and, indeed, hold implications for children yet unborn.

Scattered across many lands are people who regard a nuclear holocaust as more likely now than ever before. This belief has not been discouraged by the discovery in August 1982 of top secret papers in the Pentagon indicating that certain political leaders in the West believe that a nuclear war is winnable. Such a belief cuts the feet from any theory of mutual deterrence, depending for its effectiveness on the certainty that in a nuclear exchange there can be no winners.

Christians, whether pacifist or not, abhor war and all it entails. Nuclear war holds within it the possibility of the death of humans as a species. Yet some Christians now claim that the possession or the threat to use these weapons can be morally justified. Still others think that their actual use in a limited exchange might be acceptable. Such ideas are fairly recent in origin and require time to be absorbed and analysed. The main question confronting us is the applicability of traditional Christian thinking on war and violence, as enshrined in the 'just war' doctrine, to the use of modern nuclear weapons. Must we abandon traditional thinking? Or must we instead abandon the weapons which fall outside the limits of that thinking?

Homosexuality

It is probably true that 'the average Christian' (please forgive the phrase) holds views on homosexuality conditioned by the clear biblical statements on the subject, in short, being against it. Now, however, such an attitude is under serious challenge from what have been regarded as respectable corners of the Christian community. In the United Kingdom, Methodists have recently debated a report from their Family Life Committee which advocated the acceptance of active homosexuals as clergymen and claimed that a homosexual union based on love was consistent with the teaching of Jesus.

In the USA there is a whole new denomination of active homosexuals who profess to be evangelical and charismatic in their theology, the Metropolitan Community Church. It is said that its outreach has met with great response in the homosexual community. How ought we to react to this? Can those who say we have misread the Bible's statements possibly be right? Looking again at our attitudes can do no harm.

The articles that follow in this series may not carry the judgement of everyone who reads them. However, they are simply one person's attempt to air the issues again in Army officer circles and to initiate debate in the hope that God will lead us to deeper understanding, better reasoning, more certain pronouncements and bolder choices.

The Biological Revolution (1)

[From The Officer, *February 1983]*

It is said that the late 20th century is the age of the biological revolution because of the results of efforts to solve the problem of childlessness. The pain of longing for a child and the gradual realisation that no child will be conceived is not one to be underestimated. In the United Kingdom alone there are one million infertile married couples and eight per cent of all marriages remain childless after ten years. Again, it is claimed that between one-third and one-half of all problems of this kind are due to male infertility.

Some couples adopt, some foster, a child. Others settle for a life without children of their own and constructively redirect their time and interests. Still others pursue by all available means their quest for parenthood and it is these who are most likely to be offered the fruits of the biological revolution

The technique of artificial insemination (AI) has been with us for almost a century now. Its counterpart, artificial inovulation, is of more recent date, but is equally far reaching in its possibilities. The former may involve the use of semen collected from the husband (AIH) or from a donor (AID). There appear to be few ethical problems related to AIH. For example, it would be entirely acceptable where the husband suffers from sex-related psychological problems or perhaps faces castration because of some malignancy.

The ethics of AID are more complicated. The first recorded case was in 1884 at the Jefferson Medical College in the USA, involving a couple where the husband was infertile. The identity of the donor was not revealed, but in a letter to the journal, *Medical World,* in 1909 it was claimed there had been a successful conception. The technique was not widely used or even known until the *British Medical Journal* carried a full account in 1945. Thereafter, an Anglican Church Commission appointed by the Archbishop of Canterbury reported in 1948, recommending that the practice of AID should be made a criminal offence. A United Kingdom government report in 1960 did not go quite so far, but concluded that AID was socially undesirable (*Feversham Departmental Committee on Human Artificial Insemination*). In the past 20 years there has been a marked shift in opinion encouraged by the results (made public in 1973) of a British Medical Association inquiry under Sir John Peel.

The AID technique is medically straightforward. The donor deposits seminal fluid into a simple container. This is then delivered swiftly for immediate use or for freezing and storage. The procedures for freezing are complex, involving the use of a cryo-protective medium and liquid nitrogen. The thawing procedures are equally delicate. For the purpose of insemination the recipient will keep an accurate record of her monthly body cycle and basal body temperature so that insemination may take place near the time of ovulation, the optimal time for conception.

Demand for AID is growing. A spokesman for the British Pregnancy Advisory Service, on the launching of a nationwide AID scheme, said, 'Our service will open up a whole new era. We are expecting thousands of inquiries from women who cannot conceive because of their husbands. We would not necessarily turn away an unmarried woman who wants to have a baby by AID and the same would apply to lesbian couples.' In 1973 the *Peel Report* estimated that one-third of all couples where the husband was infertile would consider using AID. It is worth adding that infertility is not the only motivation. A husband may suffer from a hereditary disease or he may have entered a second marriage following a vasectomy. At a public lecture in June 1982, the director of an AI clinic in the United Kingdom stated that his two partners had carried out at least 1,000 AID procedures each. In France there are 12 AID centres registered by the central government. No system of registration or control exists in the United Kingdom and this is to be regretted.

Before focusing on the ethical issues involved, a word on the legal aspects. In England and Wales an AID child is illegitimate although the practice of AID is not itself illegal. In registering the birth, entry of the husband's name as the father amounts to contravention of the Registration Act 1965. In 1979 the Law Commission recommended that the mother's husband be deemed to be the legal father of an AID child (*Family Law: Illegitimacy, Working Paper No 74*). This would, of course, create anomalies in the case of an AID child born to a single or lesbian parent. In Switzerland AID is illegal. In the USA the position varies with the state, In California, Georgia and Oklahoma, AID is legal and AID children are seen as the legitimate offspring of the couple, provided that the husband consented in writing to the insemination. However, proposals to legalise AID have been rejected in Indiana, Minnesota, New York, Virginia and Wisconsin. The main difficulty resulting from legal systems not designed to cope with AID births is that of the falsification of records. It is a deceit upon the child and upon society as a whole.

Serious doubts have been raised about the ethical acceptability of AID. The longing for parenthood is natural and when unfulfilled is painful, but can we say that to fulfil that longing by any means is morally acceptable? There is scarcely any area of human life in which we grant an absolute, unconditional right to anyone to have a particular desire met. Becoming a parent is no exception. It may help to look at the issue from the point of view of each of the persons involved.

The AID couple
The pressures to have a child are socially as well as emotionally powerful. It is not hard to feel for the man who wrote to the Feversham Committee, 'I could not condemn my wife not to bear a child.' In such a case AID is seen as satisfying the wife's maternal instinct whilst at the same time successfully hiding the fact of the husband's sterility. It is arguable whether the stress of childlessness outweighs the stress of conceiving, bearing and rearing an AID child.

Professor Gordon Dunstan, a leading Anglican moral theologian at King's College, London, has said: 'If the spouses believe there is a nexus between marriage and begetting so strong and exclusive that

95

any invasion of it from without is wrong, even though extra-marital conception can be achieved without adulterous sexual union, they will not ask for AID.'

Of course, a husband cannot be condemned for wanting to please his wife, for wanting perhaps to save his marriage, for wanting a child at least 50 per cent 'theirs', for wanting to appear 'normal' to society or for wanting an heir. He has to find some means of coping with a sense of inadequacy. This sense can, however, only be intensified by the arrival of a child not his own. He may well have agreed to the insemination to make up to his wife for his (so called) failure. The child is proof positive that his wife and another man, not a party to the marriage, have succeeded where he has failed. In cases of adoption, the adopting parents share an identical relationship to the child and society knows of and approves of the husband as the social, not the genetic, father. In cases of AID, shrouded as they are in secrecy, the husband pretends to all but his wife and the medical practitioner that he is the genetic father. In fact, the donor is the father.

The wife's feelings are not less complex. She is able to bear a child and yet the man to whom she is deeply committed constitutes an impediment. Her expectation of motherhood and her expectation that her husband will be active in creating the child have both been denied. The first expectation can be satisfied only at the cost of the second. There will follow embarrassing interviews, examinations, procedures which she will resent for, after all, she is the 'normal' one. In all of this she will have to support her husband and somehow cushion his mounting sense of inadequacy. Many AID wives have reported intense feelings of guilt at their willing involvement of an outsider to the marriage. Some even refuse anaesthetics during confinement for fear of revealing involuntarily the secret of the child's origins.

Secrecy surrounds all aspects of AID procedures. Just how couples are selected or screened is not known. The need for secrecy discourages the seeking of independent assessments on suitability and so the selection is narrowly confined to the family doctor and the AI practitioner. This would seem too limited a procedure, made worse by an absence of clear criteria. No answer has been given in the United Kingdom to the questions: 'who selects?' 'who is selected?' and 'why?'.

The second part of this article will examine AID from the point of view of the donor, the child and the AI practitioner.

The Biological Revolution (2)
[From The Officer, *March 1983]*

The first part of this article outlined the technique of AID and raised certain questions from the point of view of the couple involved. Now the matter is examined in relation to other persons drawn into the procedures.

The donor

In all cases the donor remains anonymous, a shadowy figure not only behind but somehow between the couple. In France they call him 'the stranger'. No one knows how he is selected, save that often medical students are used and usually paid for their services. It has been said that he is screened for intelligence, health and a general physical resemblance to the infertile husband. Total responsibility for selection falls here upon the AI practitioner since anonymity demands that he alone be involved in choosing the donor. This selection proceeds without any external regulation of any kind. The number of offspring from each donor is unknown. Successful donors are likely to be used many times over and thus the risk of a half-brother and half-sister eventually mating is increased. Any harmful recessive genes in such a donor will spread repeatedly into the population and it has been claimed that a single donor might father not tens but hundreds of offspring.

One might wonder what motivates a donor; whether he has doubts about the rightness of his involvement; whether he has any opportunity properly to assess the implications or whether his judgement is impeded by pressure (in the case of medical students) from staff and teachers or even by the offer of pecuniary reward. What sort of man voluntarily puts himself in a position so fraught with possibilities for embarrassment, especially where there is resort to furtive measures to keep donor and recipient apart in the event of the donated material being used immediately and unfrozen? The German Lutheran theologian, Helmut Thielicke, asks, 'What degree of human degeneration or what degree of primitive underdevelopment in instincts and ideas is required to play the role of an anonymous spermator?' It is no answer to liken his action to that of a donor of blood, for blood does not carry reproductive potential.

The donor, as the biological father, turns his back on the responsibilities normally associated with parenthood and procreation. Anonymity cannot cancel responsibility. Neither can the absence of sexual intercourse. How acceptable is it in the light of Christian thinking to 'parent' a child you do not want, for whom you intend from the start to abandon all responsibility, and whose mother is a total stranger to you? The Feversham Committee reported: 'We feel that the role of the donor is of such a kind that it is liable to appeal to the abnormal and unbalanced.'

Married donors are in an even less defensible position for obvious reasons. It is not known whether AI practitioners insist that a married donor must have the prior consent of his wife to the procedure but such insistence should be a minimal requirement. It is not an answer to assert that a man's body is his own. No one has an absolute right over himself. For instance, we limit the right to abortion and we regard suicide as morally dubious. There is a sense in which a man's procreative capacity belongs to the whole of society, more particularly to his wife, his existing children, even to a possible future spouse, for no man is an island, a law unto himself.

The AID child

Clearly, an AID child is planned and wanted. That is a good start, but other factors supervene which may render the child's security less sound. Almost all AID children are unaware of their origins, for voluntary informing of the child is very rare indeed. Of those who do learn the truth it must be assumed that they discover it by accident, perhaps when a marriage breaks down. Research on a proper basis is impossible since secrecy surrounds every case. We are ignorant of the long-term sociological and psychological effects of

AID upon the children so conceived. What is clear, however, is the climate of deception in which the child is reared. AID becomes a family secret, the cause of sudden silences in conversation, warning glances behind the child's back. The legal status of the child is far from clear, but he has no right, in the United Kingdom, to be told his genetic parentage.

The medical practitioner
Here too, the ethics are made complex by diverse social attitudes and the inadequacy of the law. No official approval has been forthcoming for the practice of AID in Britain. At the same time, it is not outlawed. The churches have expressed clear disapproval (see the Report of a Working Party set up by the Free Church Federal Council and The British Council of Churches, *Choices in Childlessness*, March 1982). We still await the outcome of inquiries set up recently by the British Medical Association, the Royal College of Obstetricians and Gynaecologists and the Council for Science and Society. Present practice, in so far as it may be monitored, leaves cause for concern. We have seen that there is no common protocol for the selection of patients and donors or for the recording and publishing of data enabling objective assessment of results. At present in the United Kingdom the practitioner remains party to a legal offence (under the Registration Act 1965), to a deceit upon society and to an act of injustice toward a disadvantaged child. Professor Dunstan lists the medical practitioner's duties thus:
   – to the spouses, a duty of diagnostic vigilance;
   – to the child, a duty of utmost care in the selection of the donor;
   – to the donor, a duty not to exploit or spoil him psychologically.

Future prospects
The use of AID will increase. Its misuse will therefore increase. Clear guidelines must be worked out for all concerned and the professions must regulate the practice closely and with care. Failing this, legislation will be needed.

Many Christians will see the practice as unacceptable. It will be regarded as inimical to the marriage bond and as a real threat to the family as we know it. One leading writer in this field, Professor Robert Snowden of the Institute of Population Studies in the University of Exeter, has said: 'A woman will be able to have a child of her own without having to endure the gestation period, by a man who may or may not be her husband, or even known to her. Here, if ever, is the possibility of dispensing with the family as we know it today.'

The reference to the gestation period brings us to the counterpart of artificial insemination, artificial inovulation. This is the area of so-called 'test-tube babies' or *in vitro* fertilisation pioneered by Patrick Steptoe and Robert Edwards (*in vitro* is Latin for 'in glass' and is in distinction to *in vivo*, 'inside a living being'.) It is now possible to fertilise a woman's egg with her husband's sperm outside her body. Then, at an early stage in the development of the embryo, it is inserted into the womb in the hope that this will lead to implantation and eventually a normal delivery. Some forty children have now been born following *in vitro* fertilisation. No greater risk is involved than with a natural conception though it is too soon to know the long term effects on such children. It is also possible to collect several *ova* (eggs) and fertilise them all, using one, whilst storing the remaining embryos frozen for eventual use should implantation fail with the first. Alternatively, surplus embryos might be destroyed. This raises all kinds of ethical issues.

As with AIH, there appear to be no ethical complications with this method where it is limited to husband and wife, except for the matter of surplus embryos. It is very different, however, once a third party is introduced. Many of the problems associated with AID apply equally to this situation. The donor now is the female who makes available her *ovum* for fertilisation *in vitro* with the intention that insertion of the embryo will be into the womb of another woman not the genetic mother of the child. This permits the carrying and delivery of a child by a woman regarded as infertile. Again, genetic and social parenthood are divorced.

We are at the stage where truly bizarre possibilities are opened up: surrogate motherhood; selection from sperm banks of 'super-dads' for 'super-babies'; conceiving one's son a century after one's death; the 'cloning' of infinite sets of identical twins. The foreseeable genetic permutations are now endless. What was science fiction 10 years ago is established practice now.

The dangers lie in confusing availability with acceptability. Available knowledge is usable knowledge. Since Hiroshima we know as never before that not all knowledge is good, but that all knowledge will be used. Godly men and women will arm themselves by forethought and foresight to avert a drift into biological anarchy. They will re-emphasise the truths inherent in God's staggering declaration to Jeremiah: 'Before I formed you in the womb I knew you for my own' (Jeremiah 1:5, NEB), reminding society that people are born for a purpose, that human lives are planned by God, that marriage is his gift and he wills its sanctity to remain intact. Similarly, that sex is his gift and steps to render it redundant fall outside his plan for the human race.

Postscript

On the day following completion of this article (23 July 1982) it was announced in London by the Secretary of State for Health that the British government had decided, due to growing public and professional concern, to mount a full inquiry into all aspects of human fertilisation. The inquiry, to be chaired by the Oxford atheistic moral philosopher, Dr Mary Warnock, will have the following terms of reference:

To consider recent and potential developments in medicine and science related to human fertilisation and embryology; to consider what policies and safeguards should be applied, including consideration of the social, ethical and legal implications of these developments and to make recommendations.

The committee of inquiry will report in 1984, a year which rings with sinister overtones since George Orwell's famous book – *1984*!

The news of the inquiry is welcome, and our prayers might help its members to find the right answers.

[International Headquarters submitted substantial written evidence to the Warnock Committee which I was asked to put together in view of my role as our liaison with the British government and Parliament. We adopted a strongly principled stance on all the issues and urged caution. We asked for the children produced by these new techniques of sperm and egg donation to be given legal rights to know the identity of the donor parent. Warnock opposed this. However, in the years since then more and more countries have accorded such rights to the offspring. Where this has happened we have seen a clear reduction in the number of donors coming forward, evidencing a reluctance to become socially involved with their biological offspring and casting doubt on the claim that most donors act out of altruistic motives.]

Nuclear Warfare (1)

[From The Officer, *April 1983. All my adult life I have been conscious of the fact that I was born just a few weeks after the atomic bombs were dropped on Hiroshima and Nagasaki and am thus among the first generation of human beings to live the whole of their lives in the age of atomic/nuclear weaponry. The urgency to rid the planet of nuclear weapons has receded in recent years, party due to the disintegration of the Soviet Union. However, the issue is as relevant as it ever was. In late 2010 Helen and I, accompanied by Major Richard Gaudion and Commissioners Makoto and Kaoru Yoshida, leaders of The Salvation Army in Japan, were privileged to visit Hiroshima and to pray at the atomic holocaust memorial sites. For me this was a particularly important journey to make.]*

Sooner or later, there dawns the realisation in every person's mind that one day death will come. People learn to live with this. What we have not learned to live with is the dawning realisation that one day humans as a species may die. It is a generation since the advent of the thermonuclear bomb, but is that long enough to work out an ethic for the invention, possession, threatened use and actual use of nuclear weapons? For those of pacifist conviction weapons of mass destruction will be regarded in the same light as any other instrument of violence, that is, as morally reprehensible. For those who do not share a pacifist view, and who would accept that in certain limited circumstances war is acceptable as the lesser of two evils, it is a question of deciding whether the old criteria for determining the justness of a war can be made to apply to war carried on by nuclear means. Opinion on this question, even in Christian circles, is sharply divided.

Over several centuries Christian thinkers have evolved principles designed to limit the circumstances in which war might be waged against an enemy. These principles are enshrined in the doctrine of the just war (see *The Officer*, August 1975). This doctrine recognises that whilst peace is a goal for which Christians strive there are other goals as well, such as justice, security, freedom and the removal of exploitation and oppression. These may be achievable sometimes only at the expense of peace. The doctrine recognises that the Christian has a duty to love the enemy, but a duty also to love the enemy's victims. The doctrine holds that a war is just only if it is initiated by the proper authority within the nation, if it is mounted for a morally acceptable cause, and if the end to be achieved is the restoration of righteousness and ultimately peace itself. An absolute right of conscientious objection is recognised. Two chief principles have been worked out for regulating the manner in which a just war might be conducted. The principle of discrimination protects non-combatants by insisting that primary targets be of a military nature, and the principle of proportion insists that the only acceptable degree of force is that which is absolutely necessary for the purpose of achieving one's goal. Many commentators have said that events during the Second World War revealed the total inadequacy of the just war doctrine for modern warfare.

If such comments are true, it follows clearly that the same doctrine cannot be adequate for the age of nuclear weapons. Many moral philosophers have now rejected the just war doctrine as totally irrelevant for our times; instead they seek a code of ethics for the possession and potential use of nuclear weapons. Such an approach would seem to this writer to be fallacious. There are impulses in the lower nature of human beings which can render them creatures of unmatched ferocity. These impulses have been held in check for many generations (or at least partly in check) by an insistence on adherence to the doctrine of the just war. If modern technology has taken us well beyond our former capacities for inflicting harm upon our fellows, we ought not to be changing our ethics to fit the technology, but limiting the use of the technology to fit the well tried ethical safeguards.

How the weapons came
On 2 August 1939 Albert Einstein warned the President of the United States of America, Franklin D. Roosevelt, that the country

was engaged in scientific research into nuclear fission with far-reaching implications for warfare. The research was being conducted at the University of Chicago under the supervision of Julius Oppenheimer. By 1943 atomic fission had been achieved, plus a detonation technique and a means of successfully enclosing that technique in a conventional bomb casing. On 12 April 1945 President Roosevelt died and was succeeded by President Truman. The new President was totally ignorant of the research being carried out and only on taking office did he realise that the United States was perfecting an explosive device great enough to destroy the planet.

In July 1945 the first test was carried out in the Mexican Desert. A ball of plutonium the size of a grapefruit was set on a tower 100 feet high. The experimenters retired to a safe distance of 11 miles and detonated the plutonium. An explosion ensued equivalent to that which would have been caused by 20,000 tons of TNT. A crater 1,200 feet wide was produced and all living organisms within it ceased instantly to exist. Iron pipes four inches thick within the crater were immediately vapourised. At the moment of detonation, ground temperature was 100 million °F. This temperature is three times hotter than the estimated temperature at the core of the sun or 10,000 times hotter than the estimated temperature of the sun's surface. The men in the Mexican Desert were the first to see the satanic mushroom cloud.

It is now simply a matter of record that on 6 August 1945 an American pilot dropped the first atomic device on the Japanese city of Hiroshima. The era of conventional weapons had ended and the so-called 'balance of terror' had begun. The bomb over Hiroshima was detonated at a height of 2,000 feet. Ninety thousand buildings were destroyed including 26 fire stations and 42 hospitals. Of the 298 doctors in the city, 270 were killed. To stand even a 50 per cent chance of survival the inhabitants would have to have been one-and-a-half miles from the epicentre of the explosion. It has been estimated that the number of total instant deaths was between 90,000 and 250,000. A similar fate befell Nagasaki on 9 August

1945. Death on these two occasions was caused primarily by blast from the explosion, that is, air displacement creating winds up to a speed of 160 mph and, of course, radiation subsequent to the explosion. Even today, Japanese citizens are still dying as the result of the effects of radioactive fallout following the attacks of 1945.

In August 1949, the USSR exploded its own atom bomb, thereby initiating the arms race 'spiral'. Since then, peace has rested not on mutual trust but on mutual terror. In 1960, the ill-fated President John F. Kennedy said the world contained 30 billion tons of TNT, 10 tons per human being. By 1978, the United States had enough nuclear power to destroy each Soviet city of 100,000 people or more 41 times over! Conversely, the Soviet Union could destroy each American city of 100,000 persons or more 23 times over! In nuclear parlance this is known as 'overkill'.

The classic claim made in defence of nuclear weapons is that their existence has ensured peace for the last 38 years. Have they? Since the end of 1945 more lives have been lost in conflict than in both world wars. In the light of this, claims for nuclear weapons are watered down, and it is said that their existence has deterred, if not conventional war, then nuclear war! This is surely an absurd, circular argument. We are all supposed to be warmly grateful for the existence of nuclear weapons because they have granted us three-and-a-half decades of international security in the sense that the major powers have not formally engaged in warfare one against the other during that time, and this has been due to the knowledge that any attempt to use nuclear weapons would result in Mutual Assured Destruction (MAD).

It should be noted, however, that times change and we are no longer in even the first or second generation of nuclear weapons. We live now in the age of the neutron bomb which kills people by radiation and has a minimum blast effect. A neutron bomb can be used with much greater precision than its nuclear predecessors, thus limiting the effect upon civilian members of the population. Mutual Assured Destruction has gone and we have moved into an era in which the possibility of a limited nuclear war becomes ever more distinct. There are those who would claim that this will happen in our lifetime. No longer does a state possess nuclear weapons in order to deter a potential enemy from taking a first nuclear strike against it. The primary purpose today of nuclear weapons is to deter any attack against you, even an attack by conventional means. It is no longer the case that nuclear weapons would be used only in the overall context of an exclusively nuclear exchange. Instead, we have now the concept of the 'flexible response' by which the powers belonging to the North Atlantic Treaty Organisation (NATO) would be prepared to use nuclear weapons to repel (for example) a Soviet incursion into Western Europe by means of conventional tank weapons. This concept has made nuclear war more 'thinkable' than ever before. Indeed, governments now simply assume the feasibility of a limited nuclear war. The prospect is horrifying.

The weapons today

Those countries with nuclear arsenals of their own are the USA, the Soviet Union, France and Great Britain. It is suspected that Israel, Iraq, Pakistan, India and South Africa either have, or shortly will have, some sort of nuclear weapons capacity. The information available to the writer relates primarily to nuclear weapons held in Britain.

Britain has her own independent nuclear deterrent which is part of the NATO strategy, but she hosts other NATO forces. Her nuclear weapons are both tactical (short-range) and strategic (long-range). The following are the weapons:

Polaris: Britain has four nuclear submarines equipped with 16 Polaris missiles each. These missiles have a range of 2,880 miles. Each warhead divides into three and each has a yield of 200 kilotons (compared with the 13 kilotons at Hiroshima). Polaris missiles lack accuracy but if one hit a city centre it would kill 250,000 people.

The Chevaline System: Mr Francis Pym, when he was Secretary of State for Defence, announced that this system would be used to modernise the existing Polaris system so that the missile could be manoeuvred between firing and detonation.

Trident: In the long-term, this will replace the Polaris submarine system. By the 1990s, Britain will have purchased from the United States several submarines each of which will be the length of two soccer fields, the height of a five-storey building, the bearer of 24 ballistic missiles each carrying 14 warheads. The range will be in excess of 4,000 miles. One Trident submarine, fully armed can destroy 192 cities.

Vulcan Bombers: The Vulcan bomber force numbers 48 planes each capable of delivering four nuclear warheads with a range of 2,000 nautical miles. These were introduced in 1960 and are now considered rather aged.

The Buccaneer: There are 60 Buccaneer strike aircraft, each with a range of 500 miles and each carrying two warheads. They are thought to be highly vulnerable to enemy air-defence forces, or to a knock-out strike on an air base.

NATO Nuclear Forces based in Britain: There are 170 F-111 bombers stationed in Britain which are owned and operated by the United States. The nuclear warheads for these are provided under 'dual-key' arrangements which means that the co-operation of both Britain and the United States is necessary if the weapons are to be used. Towards the end of 1979, as a pre-arms reduction talks tactic, NATO decided to deploy 464 Cruise missiles in Europe. Some 160 of these will be based at Greenham Common, Berkshire, and at Molesworth in Cambridgeshire. Deployment is due to start in 1983, and should be completed by 1988. Also in 1979, NATO decided to deploy 108 Pershing II ballistic missiles throughout Europe. However, on 23 July 1982 the first new Pershing II missile was tested at the Kennedy Space Centre in the United States where it exploded shortly after take-off showering debris into the Atlantic. It was not carrying a nuclear warhead at the time. Problems remain to be overcome if it is to be deployed on schedule. The British Government have reluctantly admitted that there is no 'dual-key' arrangement for either Cruise or Pershing. Finally, Britain plays host to a handful of US Poseidon submarines each of which carries 16 missiles, each missile having 10 warheads.

From the foregoing, it is obvious that Britain is something of a nuclear dustbin. In his writer's view it is totally inconceivable that she would survive a nuclear war. The presence of these weapons on British soil ensures that she would be a primary target for total annihilation.

How a nuclear war might start
Firstly, a nuclear war could start by mistake. The nations frequently engage in 'war games'. Such exercises carried on without disconnecting the alert system could result in disaster. Then again, the role of computers and silicone chips in the control of nuclear weapons means that a faulty silicone chip could see a Cruise missile launched in error and Cruise missiles are un-recallable. A nuclear accident is not a possibility to be sneered at. Figures released by the Stockholm International Peace Research Institute indicate that before 1968 there were no less than 33 major US accidents involving total loss of or damage to a nuclear device. It is known that on at least five separate occasions a US missile has overshot its target and crashed near foreign soil, one landing close to Cuba in 1967. In October 1960, there was the famous incident in which the North American Air Defence Command thought that it had received early warning from Greenland of a missile attack on the United States of America. It took 15 minutes before it was realised that the American radar systems had simply echoed off the moon!

Secondly, a nuclear war could begin as the result of a deliberate act of aggression. One possibility is of a minor power without warning launching a nuclear attack on a traditional enemy. Alternatively, there must be a very strong temptation indeed for a major power to take the initiative of a first strike despite all the public statements that such a step would never be undertaken. Consider the following possibility:

110

In stage one, the United States triggers off her theatre weapons in Europe which hit and destroy Russia's long-range weapons. Simultaneously, the United States launches her long-range weapons against Russian cities. Russia's only hope of response would be her nuclear submarines around the globe and her short-range weapons. The submarines could destroy parts of the United States, but such damage would be minimal, and the short-range weapons being incapable of reaching the American mainland would destroy most of Western Europe. The result would be Russia and Europe destroyed, but the United States of America hardly touched. One wonders what it would take for such a temptation to become insurmountable.

Having looked all too briefly at the history of nuclear weapons and at some of those which are deployed primarily in Britain today, and having mentioned in outline the possible circumstances in which a war might break out, the second part of this article will discuss the effects of a nuclear attack, the current arms limitation talks in Europe, and the feasibility of applying Christian theology and ethics to the issue as a whole.

[At the conclusion of this article the Editor of The Officer *inserted the following note to readers: 'As the captain remarks, Christians are divided on the issue discussed above and not all officers will agree with the opinions of the writer. Comment is invited on this and all the ethical issues so ably raised and described by Captain Clifton.']*

Nuclear Warfare (2)

[From The Officer, *May 1983]*

To contemplate a nuclear conflict within our own lifetime is, for most of us, to think the unthinkable. What parent amongst us has not pondered a precious sleeping son or daughter and tried to guess whether that young life will end prematurely in instantaneous vaporisation or, even worse perhaps, will drain away in the lingering throes of radiation sickness? Moreover, it is not only the parent who harbours secret thoughts. Today's child does not have to be very old before he or she becomes aware of the awful possibility of a world-consuming nuclear conflagration. It is slowly being acknowledged that hitherto undetected and virtually unmeasurable damage is being done to our young people by the psychological climate created by the suggestion that we must accept as morally justifiable the obliteration of the world we know. In 1962, D.M. MacKinnon, Professor of Divinity in the University of Cambridge, said, 'None who have had any measure of responsibility for the pastoral care of young people can remain oblivious to the extent to which these issues press upon the minds of the most sensitive.' He was referring to the moral issues involved in the existence and possible use of nuclear weapons.

Children in the 1980s are no less sensitive. Even when they do not discuss the issues with their parents, they debate them with teachers. The possibility of nuclear war weighs heavily upon the minds of teenagers. There arises therefore a duty upon parents and Christian leaders to be informed and articulate about the whole question, and in turn to inform and render articulate those young people within their care. Many have found that the most effective way of coming to terms with the matter is simply to be well informed about it and to think it through calmly and responsibly. To this there are two alternatives: ignorance or panic.

During the month of September 1981, there appeared on American television screens a CBS series, *The Defence of the United*

States, which began with a simulation of a 15-megaton nuclear attack on the strategic air command near Omaha, Nebraska. The film predicted a fireball at ground level for 20 seconds and a crater three-and-a quarter miles across. The fireball would rise to 80,000 feet in less than a minute, and people 16 miles away would suffer secondhand third-degree burns. Some 35 miles away, people giving a reflex glance at the explosion would be blinded by retinal burning. There would be skull fractures, ruptured lungs, crushing injuries to the thorax, broken backs, deep lacerations and haemorrhages.

Even 12 miles away, the pressure would be enough to shatter windows into lethal slivers of glass propelled at 100 mph. With petrol stations and main services likely to be set alight, a fire storm could burn for up to eight hours at 800°C. Apart from the dead, there would be at Omaha at least 200,000 seriously injured persons and the number of these with third-degree burns would easily exceed the total number of intensive care burn beds in the whole of the United States. After six weeks the total dead would be well in excess of two million. Commenting on this series during an interview on BBC Television, Dr Jack Geiger, Professor of Community Medicine at the City College, New York, said that American nuclear shelters would be useless in such circumstances. He claimed that a 15-megaton attack would dry-roast people in shelters and cremate them.

Here in Britain, there are as yet few fall-out shelters. The official civil defence effort so far amounts to little more than urging the population to stay put and make themselves rudimentary shelters from living-room doors placed at an angle against interior walls of the house.

It is precarious to seek to predict with any accuracy the effects of a nuclear attack. So much will depend on the number of devices used, the density of the population, the height above the ground at which the explosion occurs, the prevailing weather conditions, the time of year and the amount of warning given before the attack. It is true that some effects are common to any nuclear attack, that is, blast and radiation, but there will in all probability be effects not yet contemplated.

The major causes of death will be burns from heat radiation, being crushed in buildings destroyed by blast, colliding with objects in the high winds produced by the blast, receiving lethal doses of radiation from fall-out and being burned in fires. For those who survive in the first instance, their chances of ultimate recovery from burns will be seriously reduced if they have also been exposed to radiation, since such exposure significantly reduces the capacity of one's body in blood replacement.

Calculated effects

If we take an example of a one megaton nuclear explosion in a built-up area, the blast and heat effects have been calculated as follows: the wall of an average two-storey house four miles from the explosion would be subjected to a force of more than 180 tons, and a wind of 160 mph would create fatal collisions not only between people and impelled objects, but between people and people. There would be a two second flash of heat radiation travelling at the speed of light. It would cause third-degree burns on people exposed to the flash up to a distance of five miles. Such burns would destroy the skin, and if received on more than 24 per cent of the body would certainly be fatal unless prompt specialised medical care was available. A solitary nuclear weapon could produce at least 10,000 such patients. The whole of the United States has facilities to treat no more than 2,000 cases of severe burns.

The foregoing seeks to describe the short-term damage. The long-term effects would consist of radiation-induced cancer and genetic damage to untold future generations, if any survived. The inevitable breakdown of normal civic and domestic amenities would produce unimagined shortages of food and medical facilities. Disease and starvation would be rife. Official government documents exist in Britain which predict that after a nuclear attack it would be necessary to invoke on-the-spot executions for any person found stealing food.

In June 1981 the Royal Swedish Academy of Sciences completed a two-year project designed to determine the possible consequences of a large-scale nuclear holocaust in the northern hemisphere. These findings were published in *Ambio* the official journal of the academy. A nuclear battle was assumed to have taken place on one June morning in 1985. The weather was average for June. The journal reports that 750 million people, roughly half of the population of the cities of the northern hemisphere, where the bombing would be concentrated, would die within 24 hours of the exchange, due to blast, radiation burns and fire. A further 250 million would be destined to die within a few weeks or months from radiation sickness and the expected collapse of organised medical care. Over 75 per cent of the total population of the urban northern hemisphere would die in the battle or shortly after it. This would mean 1,000 million dead.

In a sense, these findings were predictable. Less familiar are the projected effects of nuclear weapons on the atmosphere. A leading chemist from West Germany, Doctor Paul Ciutzen, stated that forests would be set ablaze over 400,000 square miles. This would all take place within the space of a few days. These forest fires would throw 200 to 400 million tons of dust and smoke into an atmosphere already choked by oil and gas vapour from the destruction of wells and oil depots, and the total result would be a heavy dark cloud round the northern hemisphere which could blot out the sunlight for months (a scenario known as 'nuclear winter'). In other words, the chaos on the ground would be taking place in semidarkness and agriculture would simply stop. Consequently, those who survived the immediate impact of the conflagration would die within a year of famine. Finally, even though the battle took place in the northern hemisphere, its impact would be felt in the southern hemisphere. Whilst the northern hemisphere has only 25 per cent of the world's population, it produces 60 to 65 per cent of the world's grain and most of the fertilisers. Without these items there would be a further 1,000 million to 3,000 million deaths from starvation in the south. The *Ambio* report concluded that from all of this it seemed far from certain that civilisation might rebuild itself.

Is there hope?

In November 1969, in the era of Richard Nixon and Henry Kissinger, there began the Strategic Arms Limitation Talks (SALT). After three years an agreement of sorts was reached between the United States and the Soviet Union on limiting nuclear arms production. On 29 June 1982 a new round of talks began in Geneva known as START (Strategic Arms Reduction Talks). Formerly the talks were about limitations, but now they are about reductions in the levels of nuclear stockpiles and this is to be welcomed. President Ronald Reagan has proposed that both the USA and the Soviet Union reduce their warhead numbers by at least one-third so that both sides hold equal amounts. The Russians have rejected the proposal as unfair. They have suggested instead a freeze for the time being on all nuclear arms production including a suspension of any steps being taken to modernise existing systems. Despite this lack of agreement right at the outset of the talks, neither side appears to be discouraged and the talks are going ahead. The American chief negotiator is Edward Rowny and his Soviet opposite number is Viktor Karpov. If ever there were names to be added to the prayer lists of Christians around the world, these are two such names.

The main hope for mankind lies in reversing the nuclear spiral so that one day the world is one large nuclear-free zone. This will take a miracle. We know of one who specialises in miracles. By the grace of God we will ponder the issues with courage and with calm resolution to think them through.

The first step is to work out our ethical position in relation to the state of affairs gripping the world in an iron fist today. The Christian will not be fooled into thinking that the issues are political only. The Holy Spirit will guide us to a recognition of the deep moral questions at the heart of the matter, questions such as: What may humans do to one another? What may they do to the world into which they were born? Are there limits to a human freedom of action? Can so-called public obligation always be accepted as a cover for morally dubious actions? Underlying any position finally adopted will be a Christian insistence that human affairs be humanely conducted, together with a Christian refusal to acquiesce in what we are told cannot be otherwise than it is. We should never forget that the thing in which we are bidden to acquiesce is man-made. What humans have made, humans can change.

The framework in which an ethic for a nuclear age will be worked out will consist of primary theological insights about the essential goodness of God's creation and the blasphemy involved in risking its annihilation. Our thinking about the conduct of international affairs will be within a framework of Christ's revelation as to the possibility of reconciling enemies, made plain for ever at Calvary. Our response to the possibility of our own nuclear death will be made in the context of the words of Jesus when he told us that our worldly enemies are not those which we ought most to fear.

Divided opinions

Already Christian opinion in the matter has begun to divide. Some believers offer ethical justifications for the possession of nuclear weapons. They defend the concept of deterrence and say that it is the duty of the government to deploy such weapons in defence of the population. Others go still further and declare that in certain circumstances even the proactive use of nuclear weapons would be morally justified. They say that this would be so in the case of a limited nuclear exchange designed to forestall a large-scale exchange. It seems to the present writer that these views are mistaken.

We ought to be very slow to join those who brand the principles of the just war doctrine as irrelevant. If we bear in mind the twin foundations of discrimination and proportion mentioned in last month's article, it will be seen immediately that the indiscriminate use of weapons of mass destruction has to be immoral in all circumstances. Indeed, the entire weight of Christian thinking would support this, but what happens to our morality if the military leaders in an enemy state conceal themselves in an inner-city bunker surrounded by the mass of the civilian population? Would it be morally justified to target a nuclear warhead at the bunker knowing that it would inevitably destroy countless innocent lives in the same city? In reality, such a situation would not exist. No military leader would use merely a single missile for the task, since all the major cities would be protected by anti-ballistic missile systems. It would therefore be necessary to launch several missiles containing several warheads each against the offending bunker. Only by such means could it be ensured that at least one warhead would find its target. Other warheads would land where they might and the destruction would be vast. It simply is not plausible to think in terms of a limited and specific use of nuclear weapons along the lines suggested in the example above.

Even if we think in terms of directing missiles at non-city targets, we still have to reckon with the risk of radioactive fallout contaminating the atmosphere for hundreds of miles around and the same contamination being carried on the wind into densely inhabited regions. The plain fact is that any nuclear strike carries with it the fierce likelihood of massive loss of civilian life and a high risk of escalation to an all-out holocaust. Those who claim that a limited nuclear strike might sometimes be morally justified should instead recognise that a limited strike can only be thought of in the context of an ultimately all-embracing conflict. In other words, there is no such thing as a discriminating use of nuclear weapons.

However, even those who recognise this sometimes claim that we ought to distinguish between: a) using the weapons; b) the mere possession or deployment of them. The argument is that it is morally acceptable to threaten to use them provided that you never actually press the button. There are difficulties with this position. It raises the question of whether or not it is immoral to intend to do an act which would be immoral if carried out in practice. The possession and threat are intended to deter the enemy from striking at you first, but the deterrent effect will bite only if the enemy believes absolutely that you intend to carry out your threat should the need to do so arise. Deterrence amounts to holding your enemy's entire civilian population as a hostage. This can never be morally acceptable. It simply will not do to argue that nuclear weapons are merely 'bluff' weapons, that they are 'weapons not to be used'. Such a claim is ridiculously naïve Granted that the Christian presenting such an argument is genuinely convinced of his own personal unwillingness to use the weapons were he in a position to take the decision, nevertheless he has to recognise that the commander of a Polaris submarine or pilot of a nuclear bomber or indeed the soldier trained as a missile-key operator will most certainly use the weapons if ordered to do so by his political leaders. Such people are trained and conditioned for precisely this eventuality. The distinction drawn between threatening to use and actually using such weapons is a fallacious one.

Personal contribution

What can individual Christians do to help? First, they will be as well informed as they are able. Next, because they love the Lord and are close to him in their daily walk, they will be calm and at peace within the depths of their souls. They will be spiritually prepared and will ensure that in the event of their worst fears being realised, they have something of spiritual worth to offer a fear paralysed neighbour. They will listen to the logical and technical points made for and against nuclear deterrence. They will see on their television screens the protest marches and the cries of a frightened public to do away with nuclear weapons once and for all. At the same time, they will realise that even though you can dismantle a warhead, you cannot dis-invent knowledge, knowledge that gives to the human race the ability to destroy itself for ever. That is why the Christian in a nuclear age will pray repeatedly not only for courage but for an articulate theology for an age in which people of the world possess in their hands an irreversible human capacity for self-genocide. Whatever shape that theology ultimately takes, we know now and will always know, that it will emanate only from the power of the cross of Jesus Christ, which proclaims the possibility of reconciliation.

Let it be said finally, that when the theology has been worked out and when the ethics have been expounded, there will yet be required of us two things: that our love for the Lord shall not wax cold even in the face of wars and rumours of wars, and that we shall never find ourselves unable or unwilling to discharge our sacred calling as salvationist evangelists and to offer to dying men and women not only pity, not only compassion, not only comfort, but the hope of eternity because of Christ who died first for them.

Homosexuality

[From The Officer, *June 1983. Here is another subject of debate, with truly practical implications, that can generate more heat than light. The stridency and division experienced in some Christian denominations by the ordination as priests and even the consecration as bishops of both women and men leading an active homosexual lifestyle has not been experienced in Salvation Army circles although naturally one can find various views being expressed. These seem never to stray far from the teachings set out in our various formal Positional Statements. It pleases me that in our ranks are fellow Salvationists, both soldiers and officers, of a homosexual orientation but who are living disciplined, celibate lives of effective service for Christ.]*

When this article was being compiled, the government in London announced to the world that the Queen's personal protection police-officer had resigned because he had been involved in a homosexual relationship. There followed days of press articles and media discussion of the rights and wrongs of the resignation. Probably a majority of the self-appointed pundits concluded that the officer need not have resigned. Probably a majority of the public, claiming no expertise but giving vent to long-held instinctive attitudes, concluded that the palace had acted wisely.

Views about homosexuality, both in its male and female manifestations, have undergone change in recent years and even the Christian community finds within it a vocal minority urging a departure from the traditional stance that homosexual acts are sinful and require confession, repentance, and forgiveness. Society as a whole is in flux regarding sexual attitudes generally, and it comes as no surprise that codes of conduct cherished by many are being subjected to close re-examination. Voices are heard objecting to any suggestion that homosexuality is a 'perversion', although clearly it is so in the sense that it departs from the created order of sexuality designed to perpetuate the human species. Some decline to use the term 'perversion', preferring instead 'deviation' to indicate that no value-judgement is being made on the morality of the actions. Yet others, usually pro-homosexuality, regard it as merely a 'variant' on the broad spectrum of human sexuality. Whatever word is used, one thing is certain, that our language has been robbed for generations to come of the proper use of the word 'gay'.

There can be no certainty about the causes of homosexuality, despite its widespread presence in many cultures, ages and civilisations. At best it may be said that its origins are found in a variety of factors: some inborn, some psychological, some physiological, some social. Modern research has concentrated on the possibility of inborn factors such as the effect of the male sex hormone, testosterone, on the central nervous system, and in turn upon adult sexual orientation. However, no conclusions have been reached. Upbringing and family circumstances have often been regarded as contributory, especially where the father is either weak or absent. In the end it is safest to say the causes are not known and that generalisations are out of place. Indeed, even about the appearance, personality and social grouping of homosexuals generalisations are misleading, although it is claimed that they readily recognise one another by a glance, a movement or a certain pitch of voice.

How widespread is homosexuality in Western society? Major research carried out by Alfred Kinsey and published in 1948 (*Sexual Behaviour in the Human Male*) concluded that 4 per cent of the male population are exclusively homosexual, but that 5-10 per cent regard themselves as 'predominantly homosexual' with 25 per cent 'incidentally homosexual'. In 1965 Michael Schofield claimed that sexual experience when young does not always indicate sexual disposition in maturity (*Sociological Aspects of Homosexuality*). He estimated that 44 per cent of non-homosexual men had homosexual experiences before the age of 21 but did not develop these after that age. No figures are available on the incidence of lesbianism but Sidney Crown, a leading psychotherapist, has pointed out that homosexual women are more faithful in their relationships than homosexual men who tend to enter casual and frequent relationships.

The official Salvation Army approach to the matter is set out in *Positional Statements* (IHQ, 1980) where a distinction is drawn between homosexual acts on the one hand and, on the other, the orientation or sexual leaning which may or may not lead to such acts. The latter is deemed 'not blameworthy'. Our official view emphasises also the following:

(a) A stable society requires stable family life.

(b) Both male and female homosexuality threaten family life.

(c) The homosexual has to be understood and helped.

(d) Help is possible from various sources but pre-eminently from Jesus Christ who can liberate the whole person if there is submission to his will.

This statement achieves the correct balance. It is compassionate without being over-indulgent; it is also realistic about the sin involved without being homophobic. The need for this balance was stressed by the American Christian writer, Dr Raymond Cox: 'The church must not only maintain her biblically based conviction that homosexuality is a sin, but must give equal, or even greater, emphasis to likewise biblically based compassion for sinners whom God loves and wants to save and transform.' Cox asks if Jesus would have changed his 'Neither do I condemn thee: go, and sin no more' (John 8:11) if the woman taken in adultery had been a man taken in homosexuality. Clearly not.

The same balance is not always evident in Christian attitudes today and has not been consistently present in the past. Augustine, in his *Confessions*, refers to Genesis 19 and to 'shameful acts against nature… to be detested and punished'. Thomas Aquinas regarded homosexual acts as the most serious of all sins of lust apart from bestiality. Martin Luther regarded sodomy as idol worship and John Calvin called it 'the fearful crime of unnatural lust'. More recently, Karl Barth (*Church Dogmatics*) has written of 'a masculinity free from women' which leads to 'corrupt emotional and finally physical desire... a sexual union which is not and cannot be genuine'. Helmut Thielicke (*The Ethics of Sex*) thinks Barth too harsh, and urges for the Church a new degree of pastoral sympathy, especially for the homosexually biased person who has not arrived at his condition through dissolute experimentation. Thielicke's view is that heterosexual sinners have no superior vantage point from which to look down on homosexual sinners.

Very recently, Christian documents have appeared in the UK as elsewhere, promoting a view of homosexuality very far from the Army's. In 1979 the Family Life Committee of the Methodist Conference published *A Christian Understanding of Human Sexuality*. The bulk of the paper spells out the following:

(a) No persons can be held responsible for their orientation, but they are responsible for the way they act.

(b) Sexuality cannot be categorised so as totally to distinguish one person from another. Rather, homosexuality should be seen as a point on a continuous spectrum of human sexuality.

(c) A pre-eminent place is given to Scripture, but precise moral guidance cannot easily be extracted directly from that source.

(d) The Christian idea of love is one in which the beloved finds fulfilment. Exploitation is excluded.

(e) If sexuality is physically expressed, the goodness or badness of the choice as to how it is expressed can be assessed only by the quality of love appropriate to a particular relationship.

(f) Personal relationships are a basic part of being human, and forming stable relationships may be an appropriate way of expressing a homosexual orientation.

(g) The morality of any such physical expression is to be assessed by the same criteria which are applied to heterosexual relationships.

(h) The only ultimate scandal is lovelessness.

Readers will understand the outcry raised in Methodist circles by this statement. Although it was not adopted at a recent Methodist Conference (June 1982) it is significant that it was produced at all. A fairly similar view is hinted at in *God's Yes to Sexuality* (1981) produced by a working party appointed by the British Council of Churches, and even the Roman Catholic community spawns dissenters. A committee of the Catholic Theological Society of America stated in 1977, contrary to the teaching of their church, that 'homosexuals have the same right to love, intimacy, and relationships as heterosexuals'.

All the liberal statements hinge upon a liberal view of the scriptural references to homosexual conduct. Indeed, the Methodist document thinks there might be no 'biblical view', and that the texts seen as binding can be dismissed as limited to their own day, outmoded by 'modern knowledge', or typical of 'Paul's Jewishness'. No mention is made that Paul's Jewishness was the seed-bed God ordained for the initial growth and consolidation of Christian thinking in its infancy.

It is a highly dangerous technique for Christians to write off the Bible in forming a Christian moral stance on any topic of current concern. It is not enough to say that 'modern knowledge' has rendered God's eternal word irrelevant. At the deepest level we have no further knowledge of homosexuality today than thousands of years ago. Even if we had, the Scriptures are very plain indeed on the subject and we depart from them at our peril.

There are five texts which directly teach that homosexual behaviour is contrary to the will of God. Leviticus 18:22 and 20:13 are unambiguous. That they are part of the Hebrew law codes does not diminish their value today any more than the value of the Ten Commandments is diminished. Romans 1:26,27 prohibits both male and female homosexual acts. This is not merely a condemnation of sexual experimentation, for in the context of Romans 1-3, Paul addresses the more general question of the unreason and unnaturalness which are the consequence of turning from God. Homosexuality is thus regarded as contrary to the law of nature, that is, human nature as God intended it. In 1 Corinthians 6:9,10, we read that unrepentant homosexuals living out their chosen lifestyle without efforts to control or reorient their appetites do not belong to the Kingdom of God. The verses do not, as has been argued, refer only to homosexual prostitutes. Finally 1 Timothy 1:8-10 endorses the earlier pronouncements.

There are, in addition, passages which imply the sinfulness of homosexual acts. Those are Genesis 19:4-9; Judges 19:22-26; 2 Peter 2:1-22 and Jude 3-23. The story of Sodom in Genesis 19 has been much discussed in homophile literature. It is argued that the sin there was not homosexuality but homosexual rape and that inhospitability is the main sin condemned. However, a Hebrew reader, knowing of Leviticus, would most certainly see the homosexual acts as depraved and the force as an aggravation of that depravity.

In concluding, we should remind ourselves again of the Army's statement 'that we should seek, in the spirit of Jesus Christ, to understand and help the homosexual'. It seems few seek psychiatric treatment in an effort to change their sexual orientation. Of those who do, few become exclusively heterosexual, but of those initially bisexual, about 50 per cent become non-homosexual in practice. However, there is better help. In *The Ideal Life* Henry Drummond says: 'Christianity professes to cure anything. The process may be slow, the discipline may be severe, but it can be done. But is it not a constitutional thing... and can that be cured? Yes, if there is anything in Christianity. If there is no provision for that, then Christianity stands convicted of being unequal to human need.'

[At the conclusion of the series, the Editor of The Officer *inserted the following generous note to readers: 'In this challenging and divided modern society, officers will be grateful to Captain Shaw Clifton for his frank, courageous and informed discussion of vital issues which confront all servants of Christ.']*

CHAPTER 8

Luther

[The 500th anniversary – quincentenary – of Martin Luther's birth fell on 10 November 1983. To mark this event The Officer *magazine graciously carried the following article from me in the November 1983 issue. I have long counted Martin Luther among my spiritual heroes. Being a man of huge girth, his physical appearance belied his razor sharp intellect. His moral and intellectual courage changed the religious face of Europe for ever. Salvationists are in direct line of spiritual descent from the history-splitting events his thinking and writings triggered.]*

The birth of a son, Martin, to Hans and Margaretta Luther at Eisleben in Germany's Saxony late in 1483 brought great joy, but for the copper miner and his wife it meant one more mouth to feed. Life was hard, but Hans was to improve his station, eventually becoming burgomaster of Eisleben. Martin's love of books came from his father who, despite his humble origins, enjoyed the company of learned men.

At 18 (1501) Martin was sent to the University of Erfurt to study law. He proved an able student, becoming Bachelor of Arts late in 1502 and Master of Arts early in 1505. That year saw a decisive event in young Luther's life. He had been visiting his parents and was returning to Erfurt when a storm broke over the village of Stotternheim. A bolt of lightning sent him to the ground and in fear for his life he cried, 'Saint Anne, help me! I will become a monk!' Luther interpreted the episode as a direct warning from God and within a month was in an Augustinian monastery. By 1507 he was ordained priest.

The Augustinians were a strictly disciplined order, specialising in university teaching. After serving his time at menial tasks, Luther was allowed to resume his academic studies. It is worth mentioning here that Luther was never a parish priest or a bishop with ecclesiastical or pastoral responsibilities. He was an academic who underwent a profound spiritual crisis of an intensely personal kind. This and its outcome coincided with events and conditions in church and state in such a manner as to bring the man eventually into direct confrontation with Rome and the awesome power of the Papacy. Rebellion was not at first in Luther's mind. The Reformation happened as the effect of many and complex causes. Luther was at its centre but he did not plan it.

The personal crisis stemmed from his growing conviction that he would never do sufficient to atone for his sins. His entry into the monastery was another, albeit a major, attempt to earn his salvation. He saw God as a judge to be feared and respected, but not loved. The Creator was absolute righteousness and justice and utterly intolerant of sin. He offered grace to do good works and grace could be obtained through the sacraments of baptism, absolution and penance. Luther's religious devotion was immense and the penances he undertook many and varied. None helped his doubts. He simply could not love God. This righteous, judgemental deity was for fearing, not loving. Luther's feelings for God at this time verged on hatred, yet he was a dutiful monk and priest.

Whilst at Erfurt, Luther met John Staupitz, vicar-general of the Augustine convents in Germany. He was to become a lifelong friend and protector. It was through his good offices that Frederick, Elector of Saxony, invited Luther in 1508 to teach in the University of Wittenberg. Here he was destined to rediscover God's word, to proclaim and to preach it. Here also the key text of the Reformation found its rightful place: 'The just shall live by faith' (Romans 1:17 AV).

In 1510 Luther visited Rome to represent the Augustinians to the Pope. The city left a lasting and unfavourable impression upon him.

On 31 October 1517 there occurred a watershed event. It happened because Pope Leo X needed money to rebuild St Peter's in Rome and thus declared a 'general indulgence'. It was taught at that time that some saints have a surplus of grace and merits on which the Church could draw. Accordingly, if payment were made toward Church funds, indulgence (pardon) was granted for sins. Fund-raising in Germany was delegated by Rome to Albert, Archbishop of Mainz, who in turn employed as his agent John Tetzel, a Dominican monk. Strange claims were made for indulgences: there was no sin so great that an indulgence could not remit it; indulgences would free even the dead from purgatory and release them into heaven! On hearing of Tetzel's activities Luther preached in Wittenberg against them. He was not unique in his opposition. Many of his contemporaries, including Holland's Erasmus, attacked indulgences as at best silly superstition and at worst blasphemy.

As a public gesture of objection to Tetzel's actions Luther pinned his famous Ninety-five Theses to the church door in Wittenberg. Such an act was normal academic practice for initiating academic debate. It was not designed as a frontal attack on Rome. Luther, in 1517, was still conservative in almost all his views. The church door served merely as the university's regular notice board. However, by 1520 Luther came to reject Rome's teaching on the authority of the Pope and of the Church, on purgatory and transubstantiation. By that year he had arrived at belief in the priesthood of all believers, but even by 1520 there were no visible changes in religious life in Germany or elsewhere. The changes were all in Luther's head.

The Theses (simply a series of short theological assertions) were not particularly outrageous. What brought them to Rome's notice was their claim that the Pope could exercise authority only over penances on earth, not in purgatory. Even this was not said with revolution or breakaway in mind. The Theses were written in Latin and addressed to fellow academics. However, in defence of them Luther found himself publishing pamphlet after pamphlet and soon he was something of a popular hero in Germany. The Theses were soon printed in German without Luther's knowledge and were very widely read. (There had in fact earlier been a Ninety-seven Theses but these were ignored by the populace.) The 95 became a popular manifesto for attacking the Church which was already under criticism for its political power-play, lack of moral stature and financial exaction. What happened between 1517 and 1520 has also to be seen in the light of the emergence of the printing press, giving Luther an audience wider than earlier critics of Rome.

In 1518 Luther was formally summoned to appear in Rome but the summons was not enforced due to Rome's political preoccupations. The following year he entered into formal public debate on the issues with Dr Johannes Eck, a professor at the University of Ingolstadt. Roland Bainton (*Here I Stand*) has described Eck as 'a man of prodigious memory, torrential fluency, and uncanny acumen'. He succeeded, over some 17 days, in getting Luther to state in public his belief that the Pope and the General Council of the Church could err in matters of faith and that the office of the Pope was not divinely instituted. That was it. Luther was a heretic and thenceforward a marked man. The debate had been a disaster, but it served to crystallise Luther's views.

The year 1520 stands out as no other in the life of Luther. In that year he produced three great Reformation treatises. In *An Address to the German Nobility* (in German) he attacked the three 'walls of the Romanists': the claim of the clergy to special grace, the claim of the Pope to exclusive authority in matters of doctrine, and the claim of the Pope that only he could summon a General Council of the Church. This work developed the doctrine of the priesthood of all believers. In *The Babylonian Captivity of the Church* (in Latin) he set out his views on sacraments and in particular on the eucharist, on which his view has been labelled 'con-substantiation' but Luther never used the term. He claimed that Christ is present in the elements, but how he is present is a mystery. In many ways this work was his most revolutionary.

In October 1520 the Pope issued a bull (Latin *bulla* – proclamation) of excommunication but gave Luther 60 days to recant. The bull was burned. There followed *The Freedom of the Christian Man* dealing with the truth of justification by grace alone through faith: 'No good work can rely upon the word of God or live in the soul, for faith alone and the word of God rule in the soul…. It is clear that a Christian has no need of works to save him; he has all he needs in faith…. Our faith in Christ does not free us from works but from false opinions concerning works, that is, from the foolish presumption that justification is acquired by works.'

Luther's relationship to the Church was still unresolved. Through the representations of his protector, the Elector of Saxony, he won the right to be heard by a 'diet', a tribunal of learned and impartial judges. So the Diet of Worms opened on 27 January, 1521. Luther had been promised safe conduct. The tribunal consisted of no less than Charles V, the Holy Roman Emperor, six electors, dukes, archbishops, bishops, princes, papal nuncios – some 200 judges in all. Luther stood before them. In short, over three days, he was repeatedly asked to recant and he repeatedly refused: 'I cannot… I will not… recant! Here I stand. I can do no other. God help me. Amen.' He left Worms, only to be kidnapped and hidden by his friends for his own safety.

By late 1521 Luther's stand resulted in visible changes in Church practice in Germany. Monks abandoned their cloisters and Luther's friend, Philip Melancthon, celebrated an evangelical Lord's Supper (without Luther's knowledge). Early in 1522 Luther returned to Wittenberg to work on his translation of the Bible into German. The Reformation was now an open and active movement for real change.

Change came quicker than Luther would have wished. Events took over. The inspiration of Luther's teaching produced practical fanaticism in some which he decried. Many priests married. Luther did so later in 1525, his bride being a former nun, Katharina von Bora. They had six children. Vestments were dispensed with. The mass was no longer referred to as a sacrifice. Images and ornaments in churches were destroyed. It took firm action by Luther to restore public order in Wittenberg. By 1526 he produced the mass in the German vernacular. Many German cities openly adopted Luther's reforms and in the next decade the impact was seen in Switzerland and Scandinavia. Rome's supremacy was ended.

Luther died where he was born, in Eisleben, on 18 February 1546. He stands, 500 years on, as an immense figure in the history of Christianity. His teaching, his preaching, his liturgy, his hymns, his Bible – all have had an immeasurable influence on non-Catholics since his day. Even the Roman Church has benefited, for it began to set its own house in order after the Lutheran Reformation. Salvationists stand in direct line of descent from Luther's teachings. They may shun the 'Protestant' label for that of 'Attestant' (witness), but history cannot be changed and because of Luther we are 'Protestant attestants' to the grace of Christ.

CHAPTER 9

Special Book Review
The Church and the Bomb – Nuclear Weapons and Christian Conscience
(Hodder and Stoughton with the Church Information Office, 1982)

[Late in 1982 this long-anticipated Church of England analysis of the morality of nuclear weapons was published. Because it advocated unilateral nuclear disarmament by the United Kingdom it received huge public attention. I was pleased that The Salvation Army was willing to analyse it through the pages of The Officer, *further signaling our growing readiness to engage with pressing moral issues. The review article was sub-headed: 'Captain Shaw Clifton reviews a controversial book.']*

Nuclear weapons constitute the greatest moral issue of our times. If we get the ethics wrong on this one, all other moral issues become simply a matter of history – if there is anyone around to write it or read it. *The Church and the Bomb* is not just one more document in the nuclear debate but is a major statement from a Christian source and, in the United Kingdom at least, has hit the headlines.

In July 1979 the General Synod of the Church of England instructed its Board for Social Responsibility 'to study the implications for Christian discipleship of the acceptance... of nuclear weapons', and now, after two years of study, the working party has offered its conclusions as 'a helpful guide in the valley of decision'. The group was chaired by the Bishop of Salisbury, John Austin Baker, regarded widely as perhaps the leading Anglican thinker of our day. Five other distinguished members made up the group, including the Quaker, Sydney D. Bailey, author of *Prohibitions and Restraints in War*. Although the members were selected initially to represent a cross-section of opinion in Christian circles, they have unanimously agreed their conclusions.

In short, the report concludes that the United Kingdom should, on both political and moral grounds, abandon all nuclear weapons. This clearly articulated 'unilateralist' stance has aroused much adverse criticism from sources in government and from Christians both inside and outside Anglicanism. In particular, the Board for Social Responsibility, which commissioned the report in the first place, has distanced itself from it. The Board's Chairman, Dr Graham Leonard, Bishop of London, has spoken publicly against its findings, stressing that it does not represent the official view of the established church in England. The Anglican Synod will debate the report early in 1983. Present indications are that the Anglican bishops, clergy and laity are all evenly divided on the issue.

The document is immensely readable, for it assumes no prior knowledge and offers all the basic scientific data before embarking on the theological and ethical considerations. The conclusions and recommendations are concisely set out in a final chapter. Despite the relative simplicity of the report, the complexity of the issues is never ignored. The working party must be congratulated on the presentation of very complicated moral arguments in a manner which makes them intelligible to non-experts. There is a most useful glossary, but the absence of an index is a defect.

The report dodges none of the issues. It explicitly denies it is a pacifist document. It explores at length Soviet foreign policy intentions, concluding – some might say unconvincingly – that the Union of Soviet Socialist Republics does not see war as a means of expanding its territory but maintains its vast military machine for defence if war should come and for keeping its 'client states' in line.

Most importantly, the report urges that 'the cause of right cannot be upheld by fighting a nuclear war' since the upholder of right thereby inflicts massive evil on his opponent and assures the destruction of his own state and society on whose behalf he seeks to protect the right. The moral challenge of this dilemma, says the report, 'is new in human history'.

The recommendation that 'the United Kingdom should renounce its independent nuclear deterrent' is boldly stated and courageously argued. The authors prophesy that this would 'put new life' into the search for an effective non-proliferation treaty whilst giving the United Kingdom immense moral authority in the quest to rid the earth of the nuclear curse. There are in all 22 specific recommendations, including four which are addressed to the churches. Here the authors rightly assert, 'It is humanity that created the nuclear weapons crisis, not a malign fate or some ineluctable evolutionary tendency, and therefore humanity can overcome it. The situation is not hopeless.'

Do buy and read this document. The first step on the long road towards solving the issue is to be informed about it. It would be naïve to think that everyone will endorse the conclusions, but it is a thoughtful, balanced and brave statement, deserving widespread attention. It is battened down with sound Christian theology and points the way to hope, where all too often we allow ourselves to succumb to gloom.

CHAPTER 10

Heresies Old and New: Apollinarianism and Nestorianism

[In 1984 The Officer magazine carried a series on Christian heresies and I was kindly invited by the Editor, Major Clifford Kew, to contribute. I did so with a glad heart for the invitation allowed a further opportunity to cast off the stereotypical sole label of 'lawyer' that so many automatically attached – and still attach – to me and which not a few sadly found intimidating even though they had never previously met me or had dealings with me. I decided to make the article an imaginary three-way conversation.]

The following conversation just might have been overheard, if Captain Thinkthrough, a modern Salvationist, had been able to meet in person two distinguished fellow-thinkers from the past:

Captain Thinkthrough: I feel very honoured, gentlemen, to be speaking to you. The General has asked me to convey his greetings and doesn't mind in the least our getting together, even though you have both been branded as 'heretics'. Probably the good Lord would not hand out labels like this as quickly as some of his servants! Perhaps you could tell me a little about yourselves.

Apollinarius: How kind! I know I speak also for Nestorius here in saying how fascinating it is for us to meet a Salvationist, indeed to meet anyone from the 20th century! To think that the gospel is still preached and believed! When I became Bishop of Laodicea in AD

360 I would hardly have dared to hope that the message of Christ would still be reaching people 16 centuries later. The treatment I received from so-called Christians left me despairing for the future of the Church. My teaching was condemned by a synod at Rome and in 375 I left the Church altogether. I was openly accused of heresy and yet I loved the Lord so much I was ready to suffer for him. I died in 390 with hardly a friend. I'll let Nestorius tell his own story.

Nestorius: I was also a bishop of the Church, in Constantinople, but don't let that impress you unduly. When I died, I too was an outcast. That was in 451. Emperor Theodosius II had seemingly taken note of my reputation as a teacher and preacher when he made me a bishop. I proceeded to penalise the followers of Arius for their heresy, only to be accused of heresy myself. I remember preaching a series of sermons in 429 on the doctrine of the incarnation and that sparked off the trouble. You may have heard of Eusebius. Well, he took great exception to my views and so did Cyril of Alexandria. They were good men but they made it tough for me and in the end I was banished to Egypt where my life was hardly ever out of danger. Happily, the Lord is kinder than some who serve him.

Captain Thinkthrough: But what was it that gave such grave offence? Did you challenge the Church? Did you deny the Holy Spirit? What was your crime?

Apollinarius: We both taught things concerning Christ which failed to find acceptance with the majority of our colleagues. My own views have been described as 'the first great Christological heresy'. Then came Nestorius two or three generations later with different but equally unacceptable views. In the end they thrashed out the issues at Chalcedon in the great Council of 451. Had it not been for us, the issues might never have been sharply focused and resolved when they were. I suppose the Church owes us that much.

Captain Thinkthrough: Briefly, tell me what you taught about the incarnation of our Lord.

Apollinarius: Well, I regarded man as a unity made up of three parts: body, soul and spirit. You would call the spirit the will or the intelligence, that part of man which gives him the power of self-determination. Now, the human spirit (or psyche, to use your modern jargon) is invariably liable to sin and capable at its best of only tentative efforts toward goodness. It follows that we cannot say Christ had a human spirit or psyche because that would threaten our belief that he lived a sinless life. If we are to preserve his sinlessness, we must agree that in the incarnation he assumed a human body, a human soul, but not a human mind. This was replaced by the divine Logos. He had the mind or psyche of God.

Captain Thinkthrough: Now I see why your enemies were upset! I follow your logic, but it does seem to get us to the wrong answer.

Apollinarius: Our doctrine must be logical if it is to make sense. Logic further compelled me to my conclusion because we cannot regard Christ as having two minds, one human and one divine. That would be a sort of schizophrenia, if I can borrow another of your lovely modern terms! True unity of the divine and the human can only take place if one or other gives up something, since the two perfect beings, retaining all their attributes, cannot become one. Something has to go. In this case, what goes is the human psyche. That way we can preserve Christ's unity and sinlessness. The divine mind glorified the human body, making it worthy of our worship and adoration.

Nestorius: Perhaps I could ask you, Apollinarius, whether you thought that Christ developed in his moral understanding, between childhood and manhood.

Apollinarius: A fair point. I taught that he did not. He had the mind of God from the start.

Captain Thinkthrough: This is something we still debate, mostly in private discussion. We certainly no longer brand people as heretics for their views on it. But you seem to make Christ less than fully human, whereas when I read the gospels he comes through to me on very much a human level. I find him sharing my own weakness and weariness, except that he did not sin. He knew joy and sorrow as I do. He was entirely a man. If he was not, then what use is he to me

139

as an example? How can I possibly emulate his divine mind? You seem to be giving him an unfair advantage over the rest of us and yet asking us to be like he was. And what about Calvary? Did his divine mind die there? His death redeems me, yet you say he did not share the humanity of the mind. Then did he die to redeem all of me except my mind?

Apollinarius: You are right to criticise. I see it differently now, of course, but at the time the logic was compelling.

Captain Thinkthrough: Logic helps us to find the truth but it is not the only path. Some say logic is only one of truth's many faces. Indeed, the gospel is true, but where is the logic in God becoming man and dying for people like us?

Apollinarius: But you see, John 1:14 tells us that it was the Word, the Logos, which became flesh. This lent support to my teaching.

Captain Thinkthrough: Yes, but 'flesh' here means more than just the human body. It means Christ took on human nature in its entirety: body, soul and spirit or mind. It strikes me that your views leave Christ as neither man nor God rather than both man and God. You make him something of a freak, parading as a man and yet not a man. Chalcedon got it right – fully God and fully man. We have it written now into our Salvation Army articles of faith.

Nestorius: Captain, you have the advantage of arriving in the world after the major doctrinal issues facing the early Christians had been hammered out. We were less fortunate. We played our part as led by our consciences and paid the price.

Captain Thinkthrough: I recognise gladly the part you played. Tell me more about yours, Nestorius.

Nestorius: Well, I was keen to avoid the mistakes of the Arians who regarded Christ as having no human soul but instead a divine nature somehow united with a human body. My friend here, Apollinarius, fell into a similar trap and gave Christ a divine – but not a human – mind. I was anxious not to lose sight of Christ's utter humanity. You, Captain, have reminded us of the New Testament evidence for our Lord's human limitations and I entirely agree. I taught that Jesus had a human body, mind and soul and that the divine nature took possession of these. I found it impossible to accept that there was a total unification of humanity and divinity in the person of Christ. I regarded the two natures as distinct, independent and physically incapable of union in some sort of God-man. I preferred to see the relation between the human and divine in Christ as a 'junction' rather than a 'union'. This upset a lot of people.

Apollinarius: Whereas I overstressed his divinity, you gave too much emphasis to his humanity.

Nestorius: So it now appears. But I just could not see how Mary could mother a divine Person. I said that she was the mother only of that which was human in Christ and that it was ludicrous to suggest she had borne a son who was divine, eternal and therefore older than herself!

Captain Thinkthrough: Again, your logic carried you too far. You sound to me as if you were saying there were two Persons in Christ, one human, one divine. Today we speak of only one Person, but two natures.

Nestorius: I know. They accused me also of preaching adoptionism, the idea that God found Jesus, a good and holy man, and bestowed divinity on him as a reward. Perhaps I failed to make myself clear, for that was not my view. My principal aim was to hold intact Christ's humanity. I could not see it depleted for the sake of divinity like Apollinarius here. I even went so far as to teach that God incarnate did not die at Calvary. Only the human Christ died, to be raised up by God incarnate. But then they said I was detracting from the completeness of God's self-giving on the cross. I replied that it was essential to see the human and divine as close but separate. I wanted to hold the natures apart but to unite our worship of them both. I saw the man as the temple indwelt by God. Perhaps my biggest fault was my failure to clarify and communicate my true thinking,

Apollinarius: Maybe we are both to blame on that score. Anyway, the Council of Chalcedon sorted it all out in 451. It affirmed both

141

the full deity and the full humanity of Christ, saying he was 'perfect in Godhead' and 'perfect in manhood, truly God and truly man… of one substance with the Father as touching the Godhead, of one substance with us as touching the manhood, like us in all things apart from sin'.

Captain Thinkthrough: We still find it far from easy to grasp all this. The Chalcedonian definitions assert the two natures of Christ 'without confusion, without change, without division, without separation… concurring in one Person' and the Army reflects this in its fourth article of faith. It is when we try to figure out how this can be, just by what means such union of two separate natures is achieved, that we begin to lose our way, as you two seem to have done.

Nestorius: We know now that there is no answer to that question. We are left only with a miracle and a mystery. It is all beyond the power of the human mind, transcending logic.

Captain Thinkthrough: I am sure that is right. Yet we still have those whose questioning, adventurous minds lead them into the risk of error. We are kinder to them these days for their motives are to restate Christian beliefs in 20th century, instead of fifth-century, language. Perhaps one day they will succeed, but in the meantime we teach the truths affirmed at Chalcedon. Gentlemen, it is time to go. How about a prayer together for Christian thinkers and teachers everywhere?

CHAPTER 11

Our Legal Machinery:
A Short Review of Army Constitutions
Worldwide

[In the issues for July and August 1989 The Officer *magazine carried two articles from me outlining the nature of our legal and constitutional arrangements around the world. As the Legal and Parliamentary Secretary at International Headquarters it was a key part of my duties to safeguard our legal status country by country and to advise the General and other leaders accordingly. It was a role I found both stimulating and enjoyable. These articles, here merged to form a single chapter, were written toward the end of my tenure at IHQ and appeared in print just after Helen and I took up our appointments as corps officers in Bromley, London. My successor at IHQ was the then Captain Peter Smith who served well in the role for 20 years before retirement and then helped to set up a new in-house legal unit for the United Kingdom Territory. Major Peter Smith was followed in the international legal role in 2009 by Commissioner Kenneth Hodder who combines this with service as the International Secretary for Personnel. While naturally the law has changed through the years, the basic principles referred to in this chapter remain of relevance to the Army today. The occasional use of the feminine pronoun when referring to the General is because at the time of publication General Eva Burrows was in office.]*

If today we devote much time and trouble to ensuring that we work and witness for the Lord from a secure legal position country by country we are doing only what our Founder taught us by example. William Booth was never reluctant to enlist the law in the cause of the Kingdom.

After first drawing up a set of rules in 1870 for the Christian Mission, he then set his hand, with George Scott Railton, to a Deed of 15 June 1875 as 'President or Chairman of Conference'. The Deed spelt out the trusts on which property was held, recited 'what are and shall be for ever the doctrines' of the Mission, and established Booth as General Superintendent 'for the term of his natural life' with power to name his own successor. Three years later he and Railton annulled the document and executed in its place the historical Deed of Constitution of 7 August 1878 giving Booth even wider powers for 'the oversight direction and control' of the Mission (the phrase quoted having survived into the Salvation Army Act 1980). On 26 July 1904 a further Deed provided in certain circumstances for the convening of 'the High Council of The Salvation Army', and in the meantime yet another Deed brought into being the watershed Darkest England Scheme on 30 January 1891.

Such measures, born of a readiness to turn the ways of the world and secular legal devices to the advantage of the gospel, brought legal stability and soundness to the fledgling Army. In terms of international policy, the same is done today. In each country in which God has established us we seek to operate from a firm legal base. We try to ensure that in legal terms the Army is truly indigenous to the country in question and is not regarded merely as a branch of a British organisation on foreign soil. It is an aspect of our internationalism sometimes overlooked.

In earlier years our legal constitutions from country to country were sometimes hastily adopted and little attention was given to consistency of content internationally. Present policy seeks to keep our constitutions as 'Army' as local laws will allow. When the IHQ Legal Section drafts, revises or offers opinion on constitutional documents we simply keep asking: 'Is this as yellow, red and blue as we can make it?' The three issues we examine with especial care are as follows:

1) Is it possible under local law to build into the constitution explicit and formal powers for the General? Can we build a direct link between the office of the General and the Army in the country concerned?

2) Does local law allow us to set out in full our Articles of Faith within the body of the constitution? Can we be legally explicit about who and what we are?

3) Can we lawfully make reference in the constitution to the role of our international orders and regulations? Can we state explicitly that these will be part and parcel of the legal life of the Army in the place in question?

If we succeed on all three points then we can feel sure we have a truly 'Army' legal basis. It should be noted, of course, that many of our constitutions take the form of an incorporation (a company) the form of whose Memorandum and Articles of Association will be closely circumscribed by local law so that on the face of the legal documents the only clue to our evangelical and spiritual purposes will be the name of the Army itself. The documents will be secular in terms of their main content. Thus it is necessary sometimes to modify our ambitions in relation to the three primary points listed above. However, we do so only slowly and with reluctance, and not until we are very sure indeed that local legal considerations leave us no other choice. Point 3 is found to present few difficulties around the world. Similarly, we are now producing many legal constitutions which emphasise explicitly our evangelical aims and have built into them the entire text of our doctrines (see Point 2 above). Any attempt to change the Army's doctrines would result in vast international legal complications.

It is on Point 1 that we most often have to come to some accommodation with local legal requirements. Nationalistic attitudes can prevent any overt reference to any person or authority outside a country. So if we cannot grant to the General a fully formal role in

145

a constitution, we might instead be able to state that the local legal representative can be appointed only by the General. We would also aim to give the General control over changes to the terms of the constitution and over the question of dissolving or winding-up the Army's legal existence in a particular country.

Happily, there are many instances now of Army constitutions by means of which local law empowers the General to act in person or through chosen representatives. The clearest examples are to be found in those many nation-states which make up the Caribbean Territory. The General issues powers of attorney to local Army leaders to act in her name so that their actions are, in law, the acts of the General. Other examples of the General having a direct legal link to a local Army constitution are found in countries as varied and as far apart as Austria, Taiwan, Congo, Panama, Portugal, Spain, Venezuela and Zambia. Elsewhere it is convenient to provide that legal powers will vest in certain officers who hold particular leadership appointments. A prime example is the USA where our many incorporations uniformly have as ex officio directors or trustees the national commander with the territorial commander and chief secretary of the particular territory. These three would normally be respectively Chairman, President and Vice-President of the Board of Directors/Trustees of each corporation.

The legal systems of the world offer a wide variety of legal devices of which the Army can take advantage when settling a constitution. We are not fussy about which legal animal we use, provided it can be tamed to serve the Army's needs. It is convenient for the purposes of this article to mention six broad (slightly overlapping) categories:

1. The most secure legal foundation is one that is created by *statute*. We have 25 such constitutions. They take the form of an enactment by a local parliament or legislative assembly, that statutory measure being tailored to our requirements and granting us legal status and powers backed by the highest local legal authority. No fewer than eight of these are in the Caribbean (Antigua, Bahamas, Barbados, Belize, Guyana, Jamaica, St Vincent and the Grenadines,

and Trinidad and Tobago). Others are found in Hong Kong, Kenya, Malaysia (including Sarawak), Singapore, Sri Lanka and the United Kingdom.

Each statute referred to makes the General of The Salvation Army a corporation sole in each of these countries. A corporation sole is a fairly rare legal entity whereby one person, by virtue of having been granted some office, can take and hold property to himself and his successors in that office. As the identity of the office-holder changes, the title to the property passes automatically and in perpetuity to each successor. Though rare in the international legal world, this concept continues to serve our interests well in many places, not least in the land of the Army's birth under whose laws the office of the General is deemed to be a corporation sole.

Further statutory constitutions exist as follow: in Papua New Guinea by the Salvation Army (Papua New Guinea) Property Trust Ordinance 1973; in Canada, under laws first enacted in 1909 where two corporate bodies now function for Canada East and Canada West; in Bermuda where our 1925 and 1956 enactments have recently been under review with the result that a new Salvation Army Corporation of Bermuda Bill was submitted to the Bermuda Attorney General's Department at the end of 1988 for eventual consideration by the Senate and House of Assembly; and in Australia where seven State enactments have brought into being corporate bodies known as Salvation Army Property Trusts with trustees appointed by the General.

2. The most commonly encountered type of Army constitution is *the incorporation*. We have set up corporate bodies all over the world, for example in Austria, Belgium, Brazil, Denmark, Germany, Liberia, Mexico, Norway, South Africa, Sweden, Switzerland, the United Kingdom and the USA. In many of these places we have more than one company. Switzerland has five, the UK has seven, and there are least 24 in the USA. The Army itself is regarded by some legal systems as merely an unincorporated association, in other words a group of people sharing a common goal but with no separate

or independent legal identity attaching to the group. The limitations of this can be overcome by forming a company or corporation. This brings into being a 'legal person' which has an identity in law in its own right quite apart from the legal identity of each individual member of the group. The company can own property and take legal steps to defend or further the Army's purposes.

Not all companies are of the same kind. In those countries whose legal systems have been influenced by English law it is usual to find available to us the concept of 'a company limited by guarantee'. Such a company has no share capital. This device suits the Army very well since it brings all the advantages of incorporation but removes any incurring of personal liability by its members beyond a small, nominal sum which each guarantees to contribute in the event of the company being wound up. Our constitutional arrangements benefit from this kind of company in Bangladesh, Ghana, India, Eire, Kenya, Malawi, Nigeria, Pakistan, Philippines, Tanzania, Uganda, United Kingdom, Zambia and Zimbabwe. Our American 'for no profit' corporations are conceptually close to companies limited by guarantee.

3. In certain Army territories the constitution is based upon the legal concept of *the trust*. Reference has already been made to the trusts created for us by local legislation in Australia. A trust is simply an arrangement whereby a person (the trustee) holds property for the benefit of another (the beneficiary). The trustee is obliged in law to use the property only for the purposes for which it has been vested in him. Hence, when we began work in Fiji, General Wickberg (acting through his duly appointed attorneys) set up the trust of The Work of the Salvation Army in Fiji by a formal Deed executed on 25 October 1973. This declared that Army assets in Fiji were held 'either for the general purposes... or for the social work of The Salvation Army in Fiji'. The Deed also appointed trustees and consented to their becoming an incorporation under the Charitable Trusts Ordinance of Fiji. This meant that our constitutional arrangements there paralleled those in the parent New Zealand

Territory where a Deed of 5 September 1931 by General Higgins established the trusts and trustees of The Salvation Army in New Zealand and provided for the trustees to be incorporated under the Religious and Charitable Trusts Act 1908 (later amended in 1951).

It is, however, in the United Kingdom that the concept of the trust plays the most crucial role. English law is familiar with the 'charitable trust' whose original scope was set out in the preamble to the Statute of Charitable Uses 1601. A welter of case law has built up around the words of this ancient preamble but it was in 1891 that the judges offered a classification of charitable trusts which is the nearest English law has ever come to a modern definition:

a) Trusts for the relief of poverty;

b) Trusts for the advancement of education;

c) Trusts for the advancement of religion;

d) Trusts for other purposes beneficial to the community not falling under any of the other three heads.

A trust coming within these categories attracts all the fiscal and other privileges of being a legal charity. All the main Army trusts in the United Kingdom are charitable trusts and the legal objects of the Army as defined in the Salvation Army Act 1980 (section 3) encompass all four of the categories listed above. This gives us maximum scope and flexibility for our undertakings within the broad range of the English law of charity.

4. Not synonymous with, but conceptually close to, the trust is *the foundation*, a legal concept used by the Army in parts of Europe and the Far East. In broad legal terms it falls between a commercial company on the one hand and a charitable trust on the other. It will normally have detailed rules for its internal administration and will be governed externally by local law. It will have clearly stated objects, a board of directors or trustees, and will be a non-profit organisation, holding its assets for the exclusive purpose or purposes stated in its objects clause. Our constitutions take this form in Finland, The Netherlands (see below), Indonesia, Japan, Taiwan and Korea.

5. In legal systems deriving their original inspiration from Spanish law we have been able in numerous countries to establish a legal basis taking the form of a *civil association*. Not unlike the foundations already mentioned, these associations offer a practical way of creating a legal entity to suit non-commercial, religious and philanthropic bodies like the Army. This is how we function in Argentina, the Congo, Costa Rica, Cuba, Guatemala, Mexico, Panama, Peru, Portugal, Spain, Venezuela and Zaire. This is in many ways a convenient legal device, but in some countries it is not possible to form an association without building into its structure a key role for a general assembly of all its members. It will be seen that this might sit uneasily with our accepted forms of Army governance and so care is taken at the drafting stage to define who shall be eligible for membership of the legal entity as distinct from membership of the Army. The former is normally restricted to officers and even then to the leading officers in the territory or command.

6. Finally, mention should be made of the *personeria juridica*, a concept which is useful to us in various parts of South America. Meaning literally 'legal person' or 'legal entity' it is closely related in form and purpose to the associations referred to above. Our constitutions in Bolivia, Chile, Colombia, Ecuador, Paraguay and Uruguay take this form.

The IHQ Legal Section believes that simple is beautiful. In other words we aim to make our legal arrangements around the world as straightforward as anything legal can be. We are familiar with the old jokes about lawyers thriving on complexities, but we would like to think the Army does it differently.

The fewer legal entities we have in a country the better it is. Fewer means simpler and simpler means more easily understood by non-experts. However, in the real world things do not always work that way and sometimes we find a multiplicity of legal creations making up our overall constitutional arrangements. The reasons may be technical and jurisprudential, or perhaps related to our history in a particular place.

In the USA we have found it necessary to be incorporated state by state and thus our large number of American companies. However, the articles of incorporation of the companies follow, broadly speaking, a uniform pattern and so the complexity is relatively superficial. The USA Central Territory has recently been able to merge into a single corporation (based on the laws of the State of Illinois) what had previously been, in a single territory, seven separate corporations answering to the laws of Illinois, Indiana, Kansas, Michigan, Minnesota, Missouri and Wisconsin. The advantages of the merger are self-evident.

In Mexico our constitutional arrangements (now under review) are multifaceted due to a combination of both local law and Army history, the work having been pioneered from the USA Southern Territory. We now have five separate legal bodies in existence. Three take the form of a *sociedad anonima* (*SA*) and two the form of an *association civil* (*AC*). The first three may be regarded as straightforward profit-making commercial companies. Life for them is complicated not only by tax considerations but also by Mexican laws which restrict both the role non-Mexicans may play in certain companies and who may own land in zones close to the national borders. The two civil associations have been formed more recently and are non-profit-making bodies. Again the need for dual associations is forced upon us by the nationality and landowning restrictions already mentioned. The situation is further complicated by legal disabilities applied by Mexican law to churches and religious denominations generally.

In Europe fascinating examples of multi-constitutional arrangements are found in Switzerland and in The Netherlands. The Army in Switzerland functions by a series of incorporations but in the last few years we have taken further advantage of Swiss law to set up an entirely separate legal constitution for the School for Officer Training in Basle. Readers will recall that this serves the needs of the France, Germany and Switzerland territories primarily, together with the Belgium and Italy commands. A full-blown legal association was created in December 1983 with four members, these being the three principal legal bodies governing our work in France, Germany and Switzerland plus the General of The Salvation Army as a corporation sole. Each of the three territorial member bodies appoints a leading officer to act as its proxy at general meetings of the Association. The General is lawfully entitled to attend in person and to preside over the meetings, but usually also appoints a proxy (the International Secretary for Europe) to act for her.

The rules of the association were revised last year to accommodate the legal life of the school more conveniently to the normal patterns of an Army training college, taking into account the multi-territorial factor and the direct role of the General in the constitutional structures. A new executive committee comprising ex officio members from five countries has responsibility for determining policy and is normally chaired by one of the three territorial commanders who serve in bi-annual rotation as vice-president of the association.

In The Netherlands steps have recently been taken which will transform the Army's legal basis in that country. The exercise has taken several years and its present success is due to persistence by successive territorial leaders, sensitive negotiation with the public authorities and others, and the availability of sound legal advice in The Netherlands. What was previously a constitution which failed to render the Dutch Army clearly indigenous according to Dutch law will now become a thoroughly systematic series of Dutch legal foundations (the Dutch legal form is the *Stichting*) covering every aspect of Army life and work. There will be four indigenous foundations tailor-made to suit the needs of both our administrative needs and our practical service and outreach with the Army itself registered separately as a religious denomination recognised by Netherlands law.

Our most complicated constitutional position is that in the United Kingdom. The reasons are largely historical. First came the early trusts set up by William Booth. Then The Salvation Army

Trustee Company (a company limited by guarantee) was formed to act as custodian trustee of Army assets as a consequence of the Salvation Army Act 1931 (itself a result of the 1929 generalship crisis). Other Salvation Army Acts followed in 1963 and 1968. Meanwhile certain trading companies were established which today undertake banking, insurance, travel, printing, supplies and housing activities.

The Salvation Army Act 1980 was a valiant, but not entirely successful, attempt under General Arnold Brown to bring our United Kingdom constitutional basis (and also our rules governing the election of a General) within the ambit of a single enactment. It made the Trustee Company ordinary trustee of Army assets previously vested in the General as trustee, but in order to ascertain the precise rights and duties transferred to the company reference back to the 1878 Deed of Constitution is still necessary (even though the Act revoked the Deed!). It also gave the General power to delegate any 'powers, duties and discretions' (but only to officers) and this is now routinely done. Once again of course the matters delegated and the terms of delegation cannot be discovered save by reference beyond the Act. Crucially, certain powers are delegated conditionally to provide for the ongoing leadership of the Army in a crisis. These are absolutely key parts of our international constitutional arrangements and yet cannot be discovered by reference to the Act. The same is true of other aspects of our international constitutional systems some of which relate, for example, to the tenure of the office of General. Of these the most significant provisions not found in the Act are those governing the age of retirement of the General. The Act itself makes these entirely a matter of internal Army regulations, as it does also the defining of our territories, on which in turn may hang an officer's right to be summoned to a High Council.

However, whilst the 1980 Act did not in the end streamline or simplify the process of discovering in total our constitutional position as derived from English law and enactments of the United

Kingdom parliament, nevertheless it succeeded in its primary aim of freeing the General from unduly close involvement in day-to-day decision and procedures necessary to the right administration of Army assets in the United Kingdom. At the same time its terms leave open the possibility of re-aligning our administrative structures in Britain without any real need to seek changes to the Act itself.

Deciding upon the best way forward to secure a sound legal base when we open fire in a new country can sometimes be surprisingly easy. It was in July 1987 that the IHQ Legal Section was first alerted to developments in Liberia and the existence there of 'The Salvation Army Church of Liberia'. Colonel Edward Cotterill, territorial commander for Ghana was in London and so direct consultation was possible. The first task was to find a good lawyer in Monrovia. This was done. It proved relatively easy to set up an Army corporation under the laws of Liberia. This was a 'not for profit corporation' very like our corporations in the USA from where Liberian law derives much inspiration. The Foundation meeting was held on 2 February 1988 and steps have just been completed to expand the corporation's bye-laws so that they reflect more accurately the emphases of the Army, and provide explicitly for the powers of the General.

Elsewhere things have been more complex. Readers will know that after many years of absence we are now back in French Guiana, part of the Caribbean Territory. However, legal difficulties at once presented themselves because French Guiana is a 'Department' of France. So, constitutionally speaking, our work there is governed by our legal arrangements in France. The legal devices used by us in the Caribbean nations were clearly inappropriate. These constitutional factors do not affect the day-to-day supervision of and responsibility for the work which remains fully that of territorial headquarters in Kingston. It does mean, however, that from a legal point of view Kingston acts as the agent of Paris in looking after things in French Guiana. The two headquarters co-operate as need arises and no special problems have yet come to light because of these unique arrangements.

The fledgling work in Angola, begun in 1978, offers further illustration of legal complications arising from a new opening. At the time of writing we have no formal legal constitution in Angola despite much effort to settle matters over the last five years or more. General Jarl Wahlström granted a very broad power of attorney to local and trusted leaders in connection with establishing a secure legal footing under the laws of Angola. General Burrows has written on two occasions to the President of Angola. Meanwhile the work goes on, blessed by the Lord who does not depend upon the laws of man to effect his will. An encouraging sign was given late in 1987 when Captain Pedro Passi, the regional officer, was invited by Angola's Secretary of State for Culture to sign on the Army's behalf an undertaking preparatory to legal recognition by the government. Now that full diplomatic relationships have been entered into between Angola and the United Kingdom it is likely that a fruitful outcome will soon be seen.

It is not possible to speak too highly of the quality of the help rendered to us by many of our official legal advisers around the world. These are appointed by the General from the ranks of lawyers outside the Army. There is space to name only two, as representative of them all. Mr William J. Moss of Cadwalader, Wickersham & Taft in New York is our national legal counsel in the USA and has served the Army in that capacity for perhaps as long as or longer than any other of our legal advisers. He knows our aims and our methods and loves us enough to tell us the truth about ourselves. Equally keen to keep us on the legal straight and narrow is Mr Dionisio Kaye of Laffan Mues & Kaye in Mexico City. He has only recently been appointed as our official legal adviser for Mexico but has already shown great enthusiasm for our work and considerable skill in addressing the complexities facing us under Mexican law.

It is good when our professional advisers also become our friends. We thank God for making available to us quality professional people with warm hearts and able minds who want the best for the Army and for those we serve. I believe firmly that God sends some of these folk to us. A relationship ensues which is often more than merely that of professional advisers and client. It is evidence that God is interested in seeing his work through the Army adequately safeguarded. Further evidence of this is found in those many occasions when legal difficulties facing us have appeared insurmountable, so much so that the Kingdom's interests have seemed at risk. Then suddenly, unbidden and unsolicited, a new factor appears which transforms matters and saves the day. In the last several years I have seen it happen over and over again, when our human ingenuity has failed and only prayer is left. It is his helping hand we need the most, and he has never failed.

CHAPTER 12

The Army's Attitudes to War

[Published in The Officer *magazine in April 1991, this article was based on a lunchtime lecture I gave in late 1990 at the invitation of General Eva Burrows. The event was held in a packed Bramwell Booth Memorial Hall at International Headquarters and was open to all working there, the General presiding. In August 1990 Iraq, under Saddam Hussein, invaded Kuwait in an attempt to take over her oil fields. Western powers responded with force and expelled the Iraqi invaders, forcing them back toward Baghdad. As the international tensions mounted, General Burrows felt it appropriate to air the issues of warfare in a broad way and invited me to do so, based on the researches for my doctoral thesis.]*

The General has given us an interesting opportunity today. We gather to think about Army responses to war one day after the expiration of the United Nations' deadline regarding the use of force to remove Iraqi forces from Kuwait. War could start at any moment.

Apart from the Korean and Vietnam wars in the post-war years, the Army has been caught up in three major conflicts since God called it into being under William and Catherine Booth: the Boer War (1899-1902), the First World War (1914-1918), and the Second World War (1939-1945).

Our international structure makes us unusually vulnerable in wartime. We were at work in 38 countries in 1899, in 58 by 1914, and in 97 by 1939. Rapid expansion across many national boundaries was taken as a sign of God's blessing upon our mission and the precious asset of salvationist internationalism was seen as a thing to be jealously guarded, war or no war.

Despite the Army's obvious vulnerability in wars involving nations where the Army was at work, no attempt was made to think through systematically, from an ethical point of view, what might be a Salvationist attitude to war. Certainly there was no such thing as a positional statement. We do not have one today, although there is the positional statement on conscientious objection, and a statement by General Jarl Wahlström issued for the International Year of Peace in June 1983 dealing with peace and disarmament.

To discover Army attitudes to war it is necessary to explore and analyse the historical sources, piecing things together a bit at a time. The sources reveal that three cardinal principles have governed the minds of Army leaders in wartime, although these principles have never been set down in any formal manner.

First Cardinal Principle: Souls
When the Boer War broke out in 1899 the Founder came under pressure from both pacifists and non-pacifists in the Army. Salvationists had never before found themselves opposed to one another in mortal combat and William Booth was urged by some to prohibit participation in war for all those in the ranks of the Army, on the ground that war was not consistent with the teaching of Jesus. In fact some Salvationist soldiers, and some officers, too, were unable to avoid taking part in the fighting for they were subject to military service, being reservists. Many had met the Army and been saved whilst serving in the British forces. On leaving the regular forces, their reservist commitment was not optional. In the face of this, Booth could hardly declare the Army to be a pacifist organisation. He resisted pressures to that end and stated openly that he could find no compelling authority in Scripture which required him to ban military service for Salvationists.

The Founder was equally unwilling to yield to those who thought he should tell Salvationists to take up arms in their country's hour of need. He said again that he could not find scriptural warrant for the proposition that it was a Christian duty to fight in war. He asked each eligible Salvationist to decide within the private confines of personal conscience whether he would offer for military service or not. The Army would not dictate. This is still the position today as far as military service in peacetime or in war is concerned.

Early in the Boer War, William Booth insisted repeatedly that when a war broke out, there was one overriding question for the Army: 'Are the fighting men and women ready to die? Are they saved? If not, do something about it!'

Salvationists were to put prayer first. They were to push their own war, the war of love. They were to seize new initiatives for God and the gospel. They were to go where the troops were to be found and they were to minister to the souls of the fighting forces. This above all else was to be the Army's wartime preoccupation. When later wars came, the same emphasis was evidenced by General Bramwell Booth in 1914 and by General George Carpenter in 1939. They called Salvationists to fervent and ceaseless prayer that God's will might prevail amongst the nations (notice that it was not a call to pray for victory, since one person's victory meant another person's downfall) and that opportunities for soul-winning might abound and be seized.

Second Cardinal Principle: Compassionate Good Works
The second element in the Army's responses to war is the organised, compassionate and practical outreach to the victims of the fighting and their families. William Booth simply called for wartime adaptation of what the Army was good at doing anyway. He wanted imaginative and flexible responses to the massive human need thrown up by war.

Pioneered in 1899 by Brigadier Mary Murray from the first weeks of the Boer conflict, this practical ministry grew and grew with each succeeding war. Just as the evangelical work was re-focused in wartime, so too was its social counterpart.

It manifested itself from the beginning in both large and small ways – from homes of rest for soldiers and sailors to visitation and letter-writing. The scale and variety of Army compassionate good works were immense in all three wars and took place all around the world. The secret for success was the simple and direct style of the ministry. The aim was to 'mother' the troops. Religion was not thrust upon anyone, but a word on spiritual matters was available if interest were shown.

A further crucial factor in making this work effective was the Army's determination to be as near to the fighting as the authorities would allow, and sometimes even nearer! The troops quickly recognised, in all three wars, the willingness of Salvationists to share the danger.

Third Cardinal Principle: Strict Neutrality
The two principles already referred to do not come as any surprise. They are not unexpected from an explicitly Christian body like the Army for whom soul-winning and practical compassion were in any case the peacetime mission. With the onset of war they were merely adapted to crisis conditions.

However, when this dual response is combined with the third fundamental factor in the Army's attitudes to war – that is, strict political neutrality – there emerges a unique denominational stance. No other Christian organisation has attempted such an outlook in any of the three wars. Only the Army, as a matter of official policy at its international centre, refused to pass judgement or make formal comment of any kind upon the warring parties, or to offer political or moral opinion as to the origins or course of the conflicts.

The neutralist policy was a direct result of a fear on the part of Army leaders that any other stance would place our internationalism in grave jeopardy. William Booth, Bramwell Booth and George Carpenter, the three wartime Generals, all felt unable to do other than remain silent on the main issues which pre-occupied the rest of the world. Their fears were threefold: a fear that taking sides, even morally, would risk persecution of Salvationists in other lands; a fear that the Army's work might be proscribed in those lands; and a fear that schism might be the result.

Each General saw our internationalism as a precious trust from God. Rightly so. Each felt that addressing the political/moral issues from IHQ, or even from a territorial level, would bring grave risk of a split in our international ranks. The wellspring of all policymaking at IHQ in wartime was thus the need, perceived to be overriding, to keep the Army united. It is easy in hindsight to conclude that the fears which gripped the leaders were perhaps ill-founded. Matters always look different when one is far removed from the events.

What might more fairly be said is that it is far from obvious that internationalism necessitated a neutralist posture. It is not self-evident that the only way to protect the Army was by saying nothing from IHQ that could possibly give offence in any particular part of the world.

Conscience

It is noteworthy that the policy failed utterly to take root amongst ordinary rank and file members. They followed conscience or instinct and volunteered in the wars or conscientiously objected according to their lights. At territorial level, in the USA and in Australia for example, the Army simply exercised a judgement about the justness of the cause in each World War and sided with their governments. Political or moral neutrality was never attempted. It has to be said that from time to time the finer aspects of our internationalist ideals were forgotten in those places as war excitement took hold, but at least an open and honest posture was struck.

The question presents itself as to whether William Booth regarded himself as legislating for all time and for all wars, as far as the Army is concerned, when he spoke in 1899-1902 of neutrality. Was he really imposing silence upon all his successors in office whenever a war came along? Would he not have wished the Army to seek to distinguish between the purely political comment on the one hand and moral comment on the other? That, after all, is what we do in peacetime. We address ourselves to government policy in many parts of the world when we think there is a moral issue or principle at stake.

Any expression of opinion would have to be most carefully couched in Christian and diplomatic terms, ensuring that our own people all around the world understood very plainly that a comment in defence of a Christian ethical principle or in defence of the gospel itself, even if reflecting adversely upon a particular government, was not to be taken as somehow an abandoning of Salvationists living under that government.

The present Gulf crisis

Although the Army is not at work in Arab lands *[in recent years we have opened work officially in Kuwait and in the United Arab Emirates (Dubai)]* and therefore the tensions for Army leaders experienced in previous wars are not present in the Gulf crisis, it is nevertheless entirely proper that the Chief of the Staff, on behalf of the General, should have already expressed a view upon the annexation of Kuwait, stating that we cannot condone such methods of solving problems. In the tradition of her predecessors in office the General has called the Army to prayer, but also, because as Salvationists we are enemies of none, she has called for prayer for the ruler of Iraq, as well as for all world leaders caught up in the tragedy.

Our prayers can be large in concept: that God's purposes might prevail; that the nations will know peace again; that there will be openings for the gospel; that the role of the Army will become clear. Or our prayers can be more focussed, more personal: for people we know who are in the Gulf; for our officers ministering there; for the political leaders by name.

Whatever happens in the political and military arena we know three things for certain: God is God and is not dead; Jesus Christ is the Saviour of mankind and all the nations of the world; the Holy

Spirit is at work and available to us if we ask. It is to these truths that we cling in the face of the outbreak of hostilities.

[The editor of The Officer *added the following footnote to the article: Copies of Major Clifton's doctoral dissertation, 'The Actions and Attitudes of The Salvation Army in Wartime 1899-1945', are deposited with the Army's Heritage Centre in London, the Archives and Research Centre in New York, the Catherine Booth Bible College in Winnipeg, the Army's Historical Trust in Wellington, and the Heritage Commission in Melbourne. The dissertation (135,000 words) was written for a University of London Doctor of Philosophy (PhD) degree.]*

The following quotations were published at the close of the article:
'As Salvationists, our nation, like our Master's, includes all nations' (Bramwell Booth in *The Officer* during the First World War).

'Pray for political leaders because this is God's world, to cleanse the mind of bitterness, and to lose sight of nationality in the face of the cross of Christ' (George Carpenter in *The War Cry* during the Second World War).

'Don't suppose that you are under any obligation to have any opinion as to the righteousness or otherwise of the war.... A pronouncement on its character is not required from you.... Remember that the success of British arms, however desirable it may appear to you, must and will involve great suffering, wounds and death on both sides.... Even if you have a feeling that the Boers are in any sense in the wrong, or are your enemies in this matter, you are bound to love them, to pray for them, and do your utmost to promote their well-being' (William Booth in *The War Cry* addressing Salvationists during the Boer War).

'The object of the Army is to spread the religion of Jesus Christ through the world.... We will know no man after the flesh; the distinctions and preferences of nationalities and governments, together with the disputes and differences existing between them, are not our business... which is to reconcile men to God.... On this rock, by the help of God, I have built up The Salvation Army' (William Booth in *The War Cry* during the Boer War).

'I fear that war will do its utmost to kill our sympathy with suffering, to destroy our pity for the wrongdoer, to close up the fountains of our compassion for those who injure us, and to silence our prayers for those who despitefully use our people. I am very anxious about this' (Bramwell Booth in *The War Cry* during the First World War).

'I deplore the menace of bitterness now growing manifest in the country…. Christ's prayer for enemies was perhaps the highest of all the heights to which prayer has yet led the human spirit. Can it not be our prayer, no matter to what nation we may belong?' (Bramwell Booth in *The Times*, London, during the First World War).

CHAPTER 13

My Favourite Psalms

In March - August 1992 there appeared in The Officer *magazine a six-part series from me which sought to expound a small selection of Psalms that had become meaningful to me across the years. I reproduce here three of the six, omitting the following: A Personal Psalm – Psalm 25; A Pessimist's Psalm – Psalms 42 and 43; A Passionate Psalm – Psalm 119. I find more and more in the Psalms as the years go by and have a sense that perhaps we do not make enough use of them. The series appeared during our final months at the Bromley Temple Corps, with the final article published as we took up our new roles as the leaders of the Durham and Tees Division in the north-east of England. All Bible quotations in this series are from the* Good News Bible (GNB) *except for Chapter 30 below which uses* the New International Version (NIV).

A Preacher's Psalm – Psalm 27

[From The Officer, *April 1992]*

If ever a psalm begged to be used for preaching purposes it is Psalm 27. It presents the preacher with a golden opportunity to encourage the congregation, to exhort them to a deeper faith and trust, and to remind them that even in the worst circumstances the Lord is totally reliable. It could well be that this was originally two separate psalms, the first concluding at the end of the present verse 6, which makes a good last verse. Verse 7 makes an equally good opening verse.

There is a sudden shift in mood and tone between verses 1-6 and verses 7-14. At first we encounter a person whose confidence in the Lord is strong, but from verse 7 onwards confidence has turned to fear. Happily, the final note is one of rediscovered confidence.

There never has been a congregation among whose members fear was not to be found to some extent. Part of being human is a capacity to know fear. For some, fear has been real in response to very specific circumstances. For others, the whole of life is beset with fear. Some of our people listen to us preaching week in and week out, and deep within they entertain hidden fears, some about tomorrow, others about what even the rest of that Lord's Day will bring.

Of course, we grow skilled at not letting anyone glimpse that we are afraid. Yet sometimes the seemingly most self-assured among us struggle with what Albert Orsborn called, 'the stress of secret fear' and 'the wounds from all but thee far hidden':

> 'Wash from my hands the dust of earthly striving;
> Take from my mind the stress of secret fear;
> Cleanse thou the wounds from all but thee far hidden,
> And when the waters flow let my healing appear.'

So much is fear a part of our human lot that we have developed a highly specialised vocabulary for it. From the Greek *phobos* we derive our word 'phobia' to denote an exaggerated or irrational fear. Hence:

claustrophobia, fear of confined spaces;
agoraphobia, fear of open spaces;
Russophobia, fear of Russians;
ereuphobia, fear of blushing;
phobophobia an irrational fear of fear itself!

The variety of fears seems endless. Those to whom we preach may be fearful for any reason: fear of failure, of the future, of death (or perhaps the process of dying), of illness, of loneliness, of meeting people, etc. Only the fool and the braggart denies the place that fear can occupy within us.

The central thrust of Psalm 27 is to proclaim that the antidote to fear is faith in the living God: 'The Lord is my light and my salvation; I will fear no one. The Lord protects me from all danger; I will never be afraid' (verses 1,3). The writer feels he can defy any danger, overcome any threat because the Lord guards him. These verses carry so much conviction that we can dismiss the notion that the writer is merely whistling in the dark to lift his morale.

Does verse 4 hold a clue as to his circumstances? He longs for the Temple of the Lord and for the sense of nearness to God he has found there in the past. Perhaps he is far from Jerusalem, yearning for the sanctuary and for the familiar atmosphere of adoration and praise (v6). Suddenly, however, we are plunged into pathos as we overhear the psalmist crying out to God in a series of passionate petitions:

Hear me (v7);
Be merciful (v7);
Answer me (v8);
Don't be angry with me (v9);
Don't turn me away (v9);
Don't leave me (v9);

Teach me (v11);
Lead me (v11);
Don't abandon me (v12).

These are the cries every human heart can make before God. There is no shame in this. What could be more natural than that fear should issue in crying out to God for help? Jesus did it (Mark 14:32-46). He knew better than anyone that fear and its paralysing impact can be dealt with only in the context of a living, first-hand trust in the Father.

Moreover, fear can drive us to a deeper reliance upon God. In this sense, fear is useful. Just as fear is useful in our daily living where fear of disease makes us wash; fear of being hit by a bus makes us vigilant crossing the road; fear of fire makes us careful with matches, and so on, so in the spiritual life fear can be used as a springboard to deepen our personal contact with and our dependence upon God. This was precisely the psalm-writer's experience. Taking the psalm as a whole, we see him strong at first, trusting confidently. Perhaps previous experiences have led to this. Perhaps he has come through troubles before and so verses 1-6 reflect a post-ordeal perspective.

Now new troubles strike. People are destroying his reputation (v12). Perhaps also there is family strife (v10), with his parents rejecting his version of events over against the word of the 'false witnesses' (v12). Whatever the cause, he knows he must throw himself utterly upon the Lord. This he does in the agonised petitions of verses 7-12. As he comes to God, all semblance of self-sufficiency gone, his confidence returns and he can say: 'I know that I will see the Lord's goodness in this present life' (v3). The psalmist's 'I know...' reminds us of the chorus we sing:

'I know he cares for me, for me;
I know he cares for me, for me.
I'll trust my Father in Heaven,
For I know that he cares for me.'

The Christian reader of Psalm 27 will readily leap forward, as he reads, to Romans 8:35-37 and the promise found there that nothing at all can separate us from the love of Christ. If the psalmist, not knowing Christ, could be confident despite his fears, then how much more can we take heart, for we know Christ as Lord.

A Pro-Life Psalm – Psalm 139
[From The Officer, *July 1992]*

For the deep insights it offers us about God, Psalm 139 has been called 'the greatest gem in all the Psalter'. It is a truly lovely psalm. The hymn of praise in verses 1-18 is, theologically speaking, one of the most highly developed passages of the Old Testament. Here we sense the mind and soul of a writer who has dwelt for years and years upon the truths he now expresses about God. With absolute confidence he celebrates his God-given existence. It is a pro-life psalm.

He begins by basking in the knowledge that he is known. He knows that he is known (vv1,2).God's all-seeing and searching eye has examined the psalmist's ways so closely that even in life's trivia (see the *King James Version's* 'down-sitting' and 'uprising', v2) he senses God's observation. There is no hint that he feels threatened by this. God sees and watches him, not to monitor his shortcomings or to punish, but to 'protect' (v5) with his power.

He feels the divine presence 'all round' and 'on every side' (v5). What is true for the individual life of the writer can be true for every person. Too many think of God as some vigilant watchdog ready to pounce. His omniscience and omnipresence make them fearful and resentful, but to the heart that loves and trusts God, his mighty attributes are a source of wonder and joy, a reason for being glad.

So glad is the psalmist that he ends by asking God not to stop examining his life (v23). Even the secret world of his thoughts, hidden from other people, is yielded up to God for scrutiny so that 'any evil' (v24) might be banished. Such openness to God does not depend upon our intellectual grasp of how God can know in detail every living person. The psalmist admits it is beyond his comprehension (v6), but lyrically he elaborates on God's vastness and power (vv7-12).

God is in Heaven (v8), the place of the highest heights of bliss. He is also in Sheol (v8), the place of the lowest depths of despair and hopelessness, where God is 'not remembered' and where 'no one can praise' (Psalm 6:5). Elsewhere in the Psalms, Sheol is regarded as a godless place (Psalm 88:5, 10-12) but Psalm 139 refuses to acknowledge such a limitation on the omnipresence of God. Our God cannot be shackled. He is God of east and west (v9), and God of day and night (v11). He needs no light to see by (v12). No person can escape him (v7 and Isaiah 43:13).

Now suddenly the hymn's perspective changes. From the cosmic God whose Spirit indwells the universe, we are shown that he is also the God of fine detail, creator of each individual human life. Elsewhere the Old Testament tells us that God gives life (Zechariah 12:1; Isaiah 44:2; 46:4). Now the psalmist declares that it is God who specifically enables foetal growth (vv13,15). As with wonder he recognises God's role: 'You created every part of me; you put me together in my mother's womb.' He bursts spontaneously into praise: 'I praise you... all you do is strange and wonderful' (v14).

We need not agree with those who think verse 14 originally preceded verse 13. The present sequence reveals a mind moving from a specific insight (v13), into a natural acclamation of praise (v14), and back again to a more developed restatement of the insight (vv15,16), namely that God creates us, puts us together, and forms us. Moreover, he knows us and sees us in the womb (vv15b,16a). Verses 17 and 18 again find the psalmist humble before his mysterious and mighty God. No human can plumb the depths of the mind of God.

I have called the psalm a pro-life psalm because it is a vivid celebration of simply being alive at the hands of God. In another sense it is a pro-life psalm for it is frequently cited in the abortion debate. A Christian contemplating the mounting toll of destroyed foetuses and the wider spread of permissive abortion laws worldwide will naturally want to take a view that is biblically informed. The Army tries to do this. We have never been absolutist in our stance on abortion. Psalm 139:13-16 is treated as though somehow it offers a final, clinching argument against induced abortions. It does not. These verses must be read with other scriptural statements, none of which gives a cut and dried ruling.

Ecclesiastes is a good place to begin for it helps us keep our knowledge in humble perspective: 'You can no more understand what God does than you understand how new life begins in the womb...' (11:5). The modern advance of biochemical knowledge leaves untouched the basic philosophical mystery of the origins of life.

Job 10:11,12 reinforces Psalm 139: 'You formed my body.... You have given me life.' This is taken a little further by passages like Isaiah 49:1-5 which suggests that not only does God know us and see us in the womb, but he can 'chose' and 'appoint' before we are born. Jeremiah 1:4 goes still further with its hint that God can and does plan for our lives, not only from the womb, but from before we are conceived (see *Revised Standard Version*).

Dwelling before God upon revealed truths like these is a first step in thinking biblically about an issue like abortion, though none of this tells us what to do or what not to do in any given case. It provides merely (but helpfully) a scriptural setting, with other references not mentioned here, as a background against which to make our ethical choices.

At the very least we should find ourselves deterred from claiming that we know the moment when human life begins, and perhaps encouraged to address questions more fruitful than whether or not (and if so, when) the foetus has a soul. It was James Barr who said that man does not have a soul, but rather man is a soul.

Is it odd in our day to offer thanks to God that we were not destroyed in the womb? Is this implicit in the central verses of the psalm? We share the author's celebration of being alive. With him, we know who formed us. With him, we know who knows us, and we look to that day when our knowledge of our great, mysterious, all-seeing, all-loving God will be as complete as his knowledge of us. One day the 'mirror' will clear and 'we shall see face to face' (1 Corinthians 13:12). Until that day, we rest content with whatever the Lord has let us see. This includes the insights of Psalm 139, awe-inspiring truths which seize both heart and mind.

A Pastor's Psalm – Psalm 145

[From The Officer, *August 1992. Bible quotations in this chapter are from the* New International Version (NIV).*]*

If we want a portion of Scripture to read in the homes of our people, a portion to encourage and to reassure them, we need look no further than Psalm 145. Seldom do I read the entire psalm in the course of visitation, but find it useful to select those verses which make clear statements about what God is like and what he does.

The *New International Version (NIV)* brings out the sense of these key verses rather better for pastoral use than the *Good News Bible (GNB* – see previous articles in this series). Thus we have at our disposal strong, unambiguous reminders of five basic truths about God which we can share with our people both in regular and routine pastoral contact, and in times of crisis. They are truths we all need to hear asserted often. For the writer of the psalm it was a matter of voicing them I every day' (v2).

Statement 1:
'Great is the Lord and most worthy of praise' (v3) The opening declaration is a broad and general statement as to the Lord's greatness. He is great and we are not. He has 'greatness no one can fathom' (v3), and we do not.

Verses 4-7 go on to amplify this theme, while verses 11and 12 show the psalmist's longing for the Lord's greatness to be known worldwide, a liberal attitude not always prominent among Jewish writers during the years of the exile.

We should note the linking in verse 7 of 'goodness' with 'greatness' in verse 3. The Lord's greatness does not comprise mere power, but is benevolent, self-evidently righteous (v7) and thereby 'worthy of praise' (v3). He performs 'mighty acts' (v4), but instead of these inspiring terror, the believer finds himself commending them, telling others of them (v4) and even meditating upon them (v5). Psalms 86:10,17 and 135:3, 5 also combine the Lord's 'greatness' and 'goodness'.

Statement 2:

'The Lord is gracious and compassionate, slow to anger and rich in love' (v8). This statement is so basic to the Lord's nature that elsewhere in Scripture we find similar words recorded as part, no less, of the divine name. Exodus 34 sees Moses alone on Mount Sinai. The Lord appears to him and proclaims his holy name: 'The Lord, the Lord, the compassionate and gracious God, slow to anger, abounding in love and faithfulness, maintaining love to thousands, and forgiving wickedness, rebellion and sin' (Exodus 34:6,7).

How our people need to hear this. Too many feel unforgiven. Their principal picture of God has him crouching, lying in wait to catch them out in wrongdoing.

Statement 3:

'The Lord is good to all; he has compassion on all he has made' (v 9). Once again the breadth of the psalmist's vision is striking. Here is no hint of a chosen few who benefit from God's love. The Lord is good to all. In fact this all-embracing note functions as a refrain for the whole psalm:

v9: 'all he has made';
v10: 'all you have made';
v13b: 'all he has made';
v16: 'every living thing'; and
v17: 'all he has made'.

Our people need to hear these verses over and again, so that again the realisation dawns: 'That means me'.

Statement 4:

'The Lord is faithful to all his promises and loving towards all he has made' (v13b). This reassuring, comforting claim is echoed in verse 17 where the Lord's love for 'all he has made' is linked with his being 'righteous in all his ways'. If he is morally perfect (righteous) and

174

absolutely reliable (faithful to his promises) then we need not doubt for even one fleeting moment that he loves us.

His 'unfailing love' is spoken of also in Psalm 6:4. It means his permanent commitment to us, culminating in the Father's gift of Jesus to our race. Let our people realise again with joy: 'I am a loved person, loved by the Lord.'

Statement 5:

'The Lord watches over all who love him' (v20a). Often I have seen comfort and hope dawn afresh for someone as this verse is read with quiet emphasis, and perhaps discussed briefly before prayer is offered. Can it be true? Are we really watched over? The psalm says we are, if we love the Lord.

It is a verse designed for those whose hearts are warm toward the Lord, offering the pastor an opportunity to tell the one visited that their knowledge of the Lord, and their love for him, is recognised and honoured. So in illness or family strife, in death or sorrow, in times of tension or fear, we are 'watched over' by a watchful God who needs no light to see by (Psalm 139:12). We cannot tell it to our people often enough.

Conclusion

The closing verse (v21) is the natural, spontaneous upshot of all that goes before it. Who could fail to 'speak in praise' of such a God once he is known and understood? 'Every creature' can praise him (see also Psalm 150:6) and their praise can go on 'for ever and ever'. The psalmist ends on the same resounding note with which he began (vv1,2).

Christian readers of the psalm will hear echoes here of the concluding phrases of the Lord's prayer, and perhaps of Paul's opening hymn of praise to God when writing to the church in Galatia (Galatians 1:5). Not only is our God great and good, not only gracious and loving, not only faithful and watchful, but he accepts our praises, flawed and feeble though they be.

CHAPTER 14

God the Father

[From The Officer, *June 1999. This article was written in Lahore, Pakistan. It refers to the famous painting by the Dutch artist, Rembrandt, of the return of the prodigal son. I had no idea that years later and after taking office as the General I would find myself, with Helen, standing in the Hermitage gallery and museum in Russia's St Petersburg where we were helping the geographically vast Eastern Europe Territory to celebrate 15 years since the Army re-entered Russia. The painting surprised me by its size. It is huge and fills a whole wall. I felt it dwarfed me. I stared at it for a long time, taking in every detail. The Territorial Commander, the then Colonel Barry Pobjie, noting my interest bought a small canvas copy of the painting as a gift to me. We had it beautifully framed back in London and it is on the wall of our home as I write. I used a version of this article for a keynote address at the Army's international theology symposium held at Sunbury Court, London, in late 2010. The modified title was* Our Holy Heavenly Father – Characteristics of a Holy God.*]*

God shows himself to us as a loving, heavenly Father. This is the beginning of our faith, for we start with the fact and existence of God, and then recognise God the Father as the first person in the Trinity. The Fatherhood of God is the beginning of all Christian belief about God. It pervades Christian literature because first it pervades the Scriptures. To speak of God as Father is to use the language of faith.

If we ignore for now the comparisons of God with an earthly father, we find 15 Old Testament uses of 'Father' for God, two of these directly in prayer. We are told that God is the Father of Israel (Deuteronomy 32:6; Isaiah 63:16), but nowhere does the Old Testament speak of God as the 'Father' of all humankind. He fathers only Israel. This is not a biological statement, but one of soteriology. That is, the Father saves them by a miracle of undeserved divine choice and election.

In the New Testament the writers burst forth with unreserved frequency to declare the Fatherhood of God. No fewer than 245 examples can be found of 'Father' used in a religious sense. Jesus is recorded in the Gospels using the word for God in 144 references, 100 of these in John's Gospel alone. In contrast to the Old Testament usage, Jesus nowhere calls God the Father of Israel, but prefers to speak of 'my Father' or, to the disciples, of 'your Father'. The only 'our Father' is in the Lord's Prayer, intended for use by the disciples. Jesus takes the Old Testament language of faith and moves it on, sowing the seed for the concept of a new Israel, a new chosen people.

In Paul's letters the description of God as 'Father' is found 40 times (for example, Romans 1:7; Ephesians 5:20; Colossians 1:12). He enjoys using the phrase 'the God and Father of our Lord Jesus Christ' (Romans 15:6) to emphasise that God has chosen to reveal himself through Jesus and can therefore be properly known as Father only through Jesus. Again, this Fatherhood is not of nature, but is a miracle of saving grace (Romans 8:14-17).

John's Gospel uses 'Father' as a synonym for God. We see the unique, incomparable relationship of Jesus to the Father (John 6:57; 10:30) and his complete knowledge of the Father (3:35; 16:15). It is Jesus who makes the Father known to others (1:18; 8:26-29; 14:7, 9) and who alone can therefore give his believers the status of children of God (14:16; 17:25f). The role of revealing the divine mystery of what God is like is given to Jesus and to no other. He is, as Colossians 1:15 puts it, 'the image of the invisible God'. He said: 'Anyone who has seen me has seen the Father' (John 14:9).

Colonel Henry Gariepy, in his best-selling *100 Portraits of Christ* (Victor Books, USA, 1987), puts it like this: 'When we think of God we think of Christ. He is our mental image and concept of what God is like. The imagination cannot frame a more noble picture, the intellect cannot conceive a higher concept, nor can the soul devise a more exalted image of God, than that he should be like Christ. He is God's self-disclosure.'

We now consider six aspects of the Father's self-revealed, but unsearchable, Christ-mediated character.

The Father has no gender

We would be mistaken to think of God as male, merely because he is known in the Scriptures as 'Father'. This faith language implies a different, twofold truth: that God is the origin of everything and that he is also all goodness and love – the perfect Father. The Bible can express God's parental tenderness also through the powerful image of motherhood. Isaiah 66:13 gives us the words of the Lord to Israel: 'As a mother comforts her child, so will I comfort you.' Similarly, Psalm 131 depicts the troubled soul 'stilled and quieted' by the Lord 'like a weaned child with its mother'.

Readers will know of Rembrandt's famous painting 'The Return of the Prodigal Son'. Henri Nouwen, who died in 1996 and was pastor of L'Arche Daybreak community in Toronto, has given us a most helpful meditation upon this painting in his book *The Return of the Prodigal Son – A Story of Homecoming* (Darton, Longman and Todd, London, 1994). Rembrandt has painted the father's hands toward the viewer as they enfold and caress the returning son's back and shoulders. The hands seem not to match. Nouwen writes: 'As soon as I recognised the difference between the two hands of the father, a new world of meaning opened up for me. The father is not simply a great patriarch. He is mother as well as father. He touches the son with a masculine hand and a feminine hand. He holds, and she caresses. He confirms and she consoles.'

179

Lieut-Colonel Marlene Chase, in her excellent devotional volume on Bible metaphors *Pictures from the Word* (The Salvation Army, Crest Books, USA, 1998), reminds us that God the Father is also like a mother: 'God is frequently pictured as a loving father in the Scripture, but he is also compared to a mother. The noblest characteristics of father and mother are resident in his heart – both the strong, protective love of the man, and the patient, comforting love of the woman. The first stanza of John Oxenham's poem beautifully depicts this synthesis:

> 'Father and Mother, thou,
> In thy full being are
> Justice with mercy intertwined,
> Judgement exact with love combined,
> Neither complete apart.'

Lieut-Colonel Chase also reminds us of the Jewish proverb: 'God could not be everywhere, and so he made mothers.' Faith language thus draws upon human parental experience, for parents are among God's first and foremost representatives of God to their children. Of course, human parents are fallible, so it is vital for us to remember that God transcends even the best of human parents, and also any differentiation between the sexes. He is God. He transcends both fatherhood and motherhood, but is the origin and model for both. We are in his image, not he in ours. He is neither woman nor man, but is pure Spirit in which there is no room for distinction of gender. Faith language can speak of God as Father, or liken God to a mother, or even to a husband (Hosea 2).

These lovely metaphors, however, offer no warrant for explicitly and directly addressing God as 'Mother'. Bible usage, and the habit of Jesus, set the example whereby we can and should address God as 'Father', never falling into the trap of thinking this confines him to the limits of mere maleness or separates him from the splendid personality attributes of femaleness at its best.

The Father has no gender.

The Father is loving

'God is love' we are told in 1 John 4:16, and 'so we know and rely on the love God has for us.' He inspires love in us by first loving us and completing love among us, 'so that we will have confidence on the day of judgement' (4:17). Love existed before the world was made, for Father, Son and Holy Spirit have for ever been in an interpersonal relationship of perfect, mutual love within the Trinity. This defines the meaning of love for all believers. All loves are to be measured by this Love. All genuine love springs from this Love. Further, just as God the Father loves perfectly God the Son and God the Holy Spirit, so he loves me too. Francis Schaeffer, in *The God Who Is There* (Hodder and Stoughton, UK, 1968), asks us to imagine a horizontal line depicting the love shared between the three Persons in the Godhead. To this we add a downward and vertical line to show God's love for me, a mere human. Finally, we add a further horizontal from ourselves to other people, to denote inter-human love that has its origins in the personal relationship existing between Father, Son and Holy Spirit before the world began.

Your love and my love, as believers, are thus validated, made real, affirmed and judged by perfect Trinitarian love. Unbelievers know nothing of this.

The Father is loving.

The Father is just

We look to our human fathers for fair play. No child enjoys a parent showing favouritism to another. Even when correction is administered, we can take it without bitterness if we know it is done justly. Our heavenly Father is a just and wise God: 'Oh, praise the greatness of our God! He is the Rock, his works are perfect, and all his ways are just. A faithful God who does no wrong, upright and just is he' (Deuteronomy 32:3,4). Isaiah too exults in his righteous God: 'There is no God apart from me, a righteous God and a Saviour; there is none but me' (Isaiah 45:21). God's Son, Jesus, therefore is 'just', dying for us, the 'unjust' (1 Peter 3:18, AV). Our just and righteous Father in Heaven turns our values upside down. He looks on the heart, not the outward appearance. His values and ways are not ours (Isaiah 55:8). We will never in this life attain a final understanding of them (Romans 11:33-36).

The church, the body of Christ on earth, is equally in need of an ongoing realigning of her values. The Father looks upon our systems, our polity and our work through divine eyes that appraise and evaluate according to his wisdom, not ours. R.S. Thomas, an Anglican clergyman and poet, has given us these telling and cautionary lines. Entitled *The Country Clergy*, they foresee that in eternity the deserving but unheralded of the church (of the Army) will be suitably recognised:

> I see them working in old rectories
> By the sun's light, by candlelight,
> Venerable men, their black cloth
> A little dusty, a little green
> With holy mildew. And yet their skulls,
> Ripening over so many prayers,
> Toppled into the same grave
> With oafs and yokels. They left no books,
> Memorial to their lonely thought
> In grey parishes; rather they wrote
> On men's hearts and in the minds
> Of young children sublime words
> Too soon forgotten. God in his time
> Or out of time will correct this.

The Father is just.

The Father is findable

The Father wants us to know him. Therefore he reveals himself and becomes findable, knowable and approachable. Listen to Samuel Logan Brengle on the theme of finding God. His words are recorded in Mrs Colonel Sallie Chesham's *The Brengle Treasury* (The Salvation Army, Atlanta, 1988): 'Some men despise him. Some men hate him. Some men patronise him. Some men fear him. But those who have found him, love, admire and adore him. To them he is altogether lovely and lovable. Enoch found him so that he walked 200 years with him. Noah found him and at his word spent 120 toilsome years building an ark, doubtless ridiculed by all his neighbours. Abraham found him and at his bidding left home and native land and went out to a land he knew not of. Moses found him and forsook the king's palace. David found him and called him his exceeding joy. Paul found him and in the midst of perils and sufferings and death said: "The love of Christ constraineth me." John found him and exclaimed: "God is love!"'.

In these scriptural examples we see that finding our accessible God produces profound change. Change and refinement are also the product of worship and adoration of the Father, the means whereby we come to him and enter his holy presence. Reflecting upon the beauty of worship in his *Jottings From My Journey* (The Salvation Army, Canada, 1998), Commissioner Ed Read utters this prayer:

'Open my eyes, Lord. Let me, in awe, admire and adore. May I see your face, its serenity and its strength, its joy and its compassion. So shall I know I am welcome in your presence. So these eyes, touched by grace, shall be satisfied with the sight, here and now, in part, there and then, of the unveiled splendour.'

The Father is findable.

The Father is forgiving

Jesus knew this. On the Cross he cried out: 'Father, forgive them, for they do not know what they are doing' (Luke 23:34). One of the central statements of the New Testament is found in 1 John 1:9: 'If we confess our sins, he is faithful and just and will forgive us our sins and purify us from all unrighteousness.'

The great English preacher-poet and Anglican priest John Donne (1572-1631) wrote:

'Wilt thou forgive that sin where I begun,
Which is my sin, though it were done before?
Wilt thou forgive those sins through which I run,
And do them still, though still I do deplore?
When thou hast done, thou hast not done,
For I have more.

Wilt thou forgive that sin by which I won
Others to sin, and made my sin their door?
Wilt thou forgive that sin which I did shun
A year or two, but wallowed in a score?
When thou hast done, thou hast not done,
For I have more.

I have a sin of fear, that when I've spun
My last thread, I shall perish on the shore;
Swear by thyself that at my death thy
Sun shall shine as it shines now, and heretofore;
And having done that, thou hast done,
I have no more.'

Nothing deals finally with guilt for sin except the forgiveness of a loving heavenly Father. That is why secular counselling for guilt, in the end, goes only part of the way. A sense of having failed to meet God's loving but clear standards; a feeling of uncleanness of the soul; a realisation of self-deception; an absence of inner peace: all these drove David to his knees as he poured out his poignant, fervent plea to the Father for purity and forgiveness, known to us now as Psalm 51. 'Have mercy on me, O God…. Wash away all my iniquity and cleanse me from my sin…. Create in me a pure heart, O God, and renew a steadfast spirit within me' (51:1, 2, 10).

Paul Goodliff is a tutor in pastoral counselling at St John's College in Nottingham, England and also a former chairperson of the Swanwick Conference for Pastoral Care and Counselling. In his recent book *Care in a Confused Climate-Pastoral Care and Postmodern Culture* (Darton Longman and Todd, London, 1998) he writes: 'No amount of psychological help can restore that broken relationship between the psalmist and his God, any more than it can restore ours. It is not a psychological problem but a spiritual one, and the promise of Scripture and the experience of every generation of Christians is that God does have mercy on us, he does forgive sin, and he does restore our broken relationship with him when we turn to him in repentance and faith…. We are not irredeemable, nor are we perfect, and forgiveness recognises both aspects.'

Through Jesus the Son, the Father tells us: 'Your sins are forgiven' (Luke 7:48).

The Father is forgiving.

The Father is firm

Because he loves us, the Father firmly but gently corrects and reproves us. This is a reaching out to us in our fallenness and lostness that once again reveals how much the Father cares. It is a corollary of his love. His discipline of his children flows from a pure and uncorrupt heart. He is, within himself, entirely at peace and inwardly consistent (2 Timothy 2:13). The perfect harmony and balance found at the heart of God's nature shows itself in a flawless union of love and correction toward his creatures. Discipline is one of the purposes of his word in Scripture: 'All Scripture is God-breathed and is useful for teaching, rebuking, correcting and training in righteousness, so that the man of God may be thoroughly equipped for every good work' (2 Timothy 3:16).

We hear again the exhortation of the older, experienced voice to the one yet to find his way in the world: 'My son, do not despise the Lord's discipline and do not resent his rebuke, because the Lord disciplines those he loves, and a father the son he delights in' (Proverbs 3:11,12).

England's first Poet Laureate, the great Ben Jonson (1572-1637), opened his 'Hymn to God the Father' with these verses:

'Hear me, O God!
A broken heart
Is my best part:
Use still thy rod
That I may prove
Therein thy love.

If thou hadst not
Been stern to me,
But left me free,
I had forgot
Myself and thee.

For sin's so sweet,
As minds ill bent
Rarely repent,
Until they meet
Their punishment.'

The Father is firm.

A prayer in closing:
O Father God, whose being transcends the limits of our human lives, look upon us with your perfect love, as a parent regards a cherished child. Seeking to find you, we come trusting in your justice, needing your forgiveness, and ready to receive gladly your correction. In the sacred name of Jesus, to whom we look to see the Father. Amen.